VISITING KASHMIR

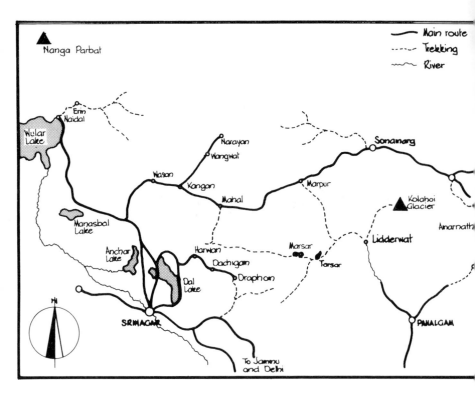

VISITING KASHMIR

Allan Stacey

B.T. Batsford Ltd   London

ISBN 0 7134 5792 9

Typeset by Servis Filmsetting Ltd, Manchester
Printed in Great Britain at
The Bath Press, Avon
for the publishers B.T. Batsford Ltd
4 Fitzhardinge Street
London W1H 0AH

For P.J.H. who shared the experiences

Acknowledgements

The author wishes to thank the Government of India Tourist Bureau for the use of the black and white photographs, and Audience Planners, St John's Studio, Church Road, Richmond, Surrey, for the use of their photographic library and for their help in photo-research. Thanks also to Peter Holloway for his advice and help in preparing the typescript and for the use of some of his colour transparencies. The maps were provided by Robert Brien. The colour transparencies were taken by the author. Special acknowledgement is due for the help given by the Kashmir Tourist Bureau, Bombay.

Contents

Introduction

After reading this book it is hoped that those who have not yet been to Kashmir will be encouraged to set off and see for themselves the place that, as for so many travellers throughout the years, represents for them a glimpse of paradise.

Here will not be found information such as timings or prices or, in the main, distances. Such information is readily available in many of the practical guides that are published. It is intended here to introduce the many facets of the state and its peoples so that a visitor will understand a complex and unusual region.

The legend that is Kashmir is an amalgamation of songs and poems and traveller's tales, plus a turbulent history, all of which date back for thousands of years. The fabled Vale of Kashmir became an immediate legend after the first traveller – or marauder – saw its jewel-like setting of lakes, rivers and islands amidst the lofty Himalayan mountains.

The Kashmir Valley is as much a delight and wonder to the present-day traveller arriving either by air or by road, as it was captivating to the Emperor Saudiman, who reigned in Kashmir for over thirty years in the middle of the twenty-fifth century BC.

One can only wonder at the fortitude of the early travellers, men such as Huien Tsang, or the painters Thomas and William Daniel. Their determination must have been supreme in order to press them ever-forward and eventually reach the Vale, settled as it is high among seemingly impenetrable mountains at the end of a route that was, and still is, full of hazards.

By comparison the journey today is easy but can still have troubles. By air, flights will not take off unless the weather forecast is a confident one, especially when flying out of season when sudden snow squalls or rising winds make air journeys uncomfortable. By road the journey is full of delays except in the summer months and can be trying to all but the most curious, those who are intent upon seeing as much as possible *en route* and have the time to spare.

A fair Kashmiri woman

Time, these days, seems to be of the essence and 'Instant Kashmir' is what the majority of tourists experience as a part of their tour. Cramming the Vale of Kashmir into a four-day visit, possibly at the tail-end of an Indian Tour, is unworthy and yet a necessity if even so short a look around this paradise on earth is to be attained.

The first European to visit the Valley, or Vale of Kashmir, was Francois

Bernier, who wrote of his extraordinary experience, in 1665, 'In truth, the Kingdom surpasses in beauty all that my warmest imaginings had anticipated'. These sentiments will be echoed by all who do go there and come away dazzled and fascinated by the difference and setting of all there is to see around the lakes and mountains.

A happy aspect of the Kashmir Valley is that it is able to satisfy the requirements of everyone. If one is hyper-active there are exhaustive facilities for using up spare energy such as trekking, swimming, skiing and climbing, to name only a few. If, on the other hand, one is only sporadically active, there are an assortment of excursions with which to punctuate a restful stay. For the really lazy the slow life on a houseboat, with sunbathing and swimming and taking numerous trips around the lake and rivers in a 'shikara' boat, is very satisfying. Those who may be infirm can also fly into the 'magic valley' and be cosseted from landing to taking off again by being taxied and rowed and cared for all of the time. Being pampered is part of a Kashmir experience, as is being pestered – by avaricious dealers. They are two of the many contrasts of life on a houseboat and are inextricably woven into the character of Kashmir.

Gazing at the magnificent Himalayas or across the translucent waters one can almost hear a voice from the past, that of Akbar the Great, who said – 'If there be a paradise on earth, this is it, this is it, this is it . . . an emerald set in pearls'.

At dawn the lakes are shrouded by a fine mist. At noon the waters coruscate with sunlight. At night the lakes are mirrors from which one can pick stars.

Kashmir is quite different from anywhere on earth. It is unique, unexpected, breathtaking and so much more than writings about it convey, or photographs show. It is as uniquely different in the way Venice is to the rest of Europe. There is no place of comparison. Be prepared, though, for having a glimpse of paradise is a tempting thing – you will wish to have another look!

1 The making of Kashmir

History

In the late second century BC the Emperor Ashoka's kingdom extended from Bengal across the Deccan to Afghanistan. In and around 250 BC he conquered Kashmir. A convert to Buddhism he made it the official religion of the whole of the region. He is credited with the founding of the city of Srinagar, originally some 6 km ($3\frac{3}{4}$ miles) north of the present city.

During his reign Ashoka established trading relations with places as far off as Egypt, Greece and China and in this time there flourished a period of building and of art and of multi-culturality.

After his death several Buddhist kings tried to control the difficult region but were thwarted by local interests, mainly those of the Nagas, the hill people, who resented interference. There followed legendary invasions by Tartars and Sythians until, in AD 525, it is reliably recorded, a Hun king, Mirikakula, ruled with 'fire and cruelty'. He sacked the Buddhist monasteries and created havoc among all the peoples of Kashmir until, in the end, he committed suicide.

One of the better-known kings of Kashmir was Lalitaditya, AD 724–760. He made war with surrounding areas, seemingly always victoriously, annexing whole tracts of the Punjab and Baltistan to his kingdom. King Lalitaditya built temples, made canals and organised drainage systems and he reclaimed land which he gave to his people. He was referred to as the 'mighty and the magnificent'. He was not without another side and could be as cruel as can most who enjoy absolute power. When drunk he ordered that the city of Srinagar be set on fire and as the flames roared he laughed insanely as he watched his folly. Eventually he died in Turkistan whilst on the march. Before he left Kashmir for the final time his most famous and unheeded edict, or law, was 'that nepotism be not tolerated', a useless utterance as it turned out. There followed a whole succession of nepotic rulers, male and female, who made or spoiled Kashmir according to their extravagances or their lack of character.

In AD 1420 the Sultan Zain ul 'Abidin commenced a peaceful and generous reign. He fostered friendship and protection for the Hindus, who had been fiercely persecuted by his predecessor. He revived Hindu learning and repaired many of the sacked temples and he granted ownership of land. Until his time Sanskrit had been the official language of the Kingdom. It was he who introduced the Persian script into Kashmir. At his court lived musicians and artists who had come from far away places, and artisans who introduced weaving, silk production and paper making, plus shawl weaving and papier-mâché work – crafts that have flourished continuously since then and are today a major contribution to the State's economy. Zain ul 'Abidin died in AD 1476, aged 69, leaving behind him the reputation of being just and enlightened and a king who had, by his wisdom and benevolence, earned for the territory of Kashmir the epithet 'the valley of happiness'.

Few were the Sultans of Kashmir who did any lasting good afterwards. Not until AD 1586, when Akbar the Great eventually defeated the last of them, did a long period of peace descend on Kashmir.

Akbar built the Fort known as Hari Parbat, now a notable and attractive landmark. He was followed by Jehangir, who created the famous Shalimar Gardens and also laid out the plans for the Nishat Bagh and Nasim Bagh (*Bagh* meaning *garden*), with their fountains and rills and cool pavilions surrounded on all sides by chenar trees and firs; each garden commanded fine views of Lake Dal and, beyond, of the Pir Panjal mountains. Shah Jehan, Jehangir's son, continued the construction of gardens so vigorously that at one time the whole of the banks of the lake seemed a continuous botanical delight.

Shah Jehan was succeeded by Aurangzeb, who showed little love for Kashmir, visited it only once, and ordered the wholesale persecution of the Brahmin Hindus, many of whom fled the country. Once again the city of Srinagar was set on fire. It must be remembered that wood was the main building material and what was not burned down eventually rotted away and therefore today little remains of the early carved wooden architecture.

In 1819, after Muslim rule came Sikh rule, Kashmir having been attacked by force by Ranjit Singh. Relief from Muslim despotism was short-lived, for the Sikhs ruled in much the same way as had others. Now even more heavily taxed, those of the people who had converted from Hinduism to Mohammedism were persecuted as Muslims by the Sikhs, even though they themselves were originally an off-shoot of Hinduism!

In 1827 a severe earthquake wrecked much of the valley and again the city of Srinagar was destroyed, as were thousands of people during the earthquake and afterwards, of cholera.

Able and relatively peaceful rule came only after the succession of

The Emperor Shah Jehan

Pratab Singh who, as eldest son, had become the Maharaja of Kashmir. He was a weak man who depended too much on the advice of others and eventually gave way to one Hari Singh who became the Maharaja of Jammu and Kashmir. This was in 1925.

At the time of transfer of power from the British Government to the newly-created Dominions of Pakistan and India the Maharaja of Kashmir, a devout Hindu, ruled over a populace that was mostly Muslim.

The frontiers of Kashmir met the newly-formed Pakistan on the west and India to the south and, harassed by both sides and in a seemingly impossible situation, after much vacillation the Maharaja signed a letter of accession of the State of Jammu and Kashmir to India; this was on 26 October 1947.

Bloodshed, looting, rape and all manner of violent protests ensued until order was restored. After Hari Singh died his son, the Yuvraj, Karan Singh, remained amidst the turmoil, first as Regent and eventually became the first elected Head of State.

It cannot be said that with the passing of the years since Independence the Kashmiri problem has eased and that a permanent peace has come to so attractive and fabled a land.

The paradox remains that a Muslim majority is ruled by a Hindu-dominated Central Government from New Delhi. Pakistan, Kashmir's western neighbour, is still laying claims to Kashmir and its borders yet India is in rightful possession of the State. These facts will be a constant in Kashmiri affairs for a long time to come and one hopes that recent negotiations will obtain some lasting solution.

The majority of Kashmiri Muslims, either for trading considerations or for tenure rights, would continue to accept the present situation, that of rule under the Constitutional Democracy that is India. The minority voices of Muslim fundamentalists who see it as their duty to fight if not for a merger with Pakistan, then for an independent Muslim country, are increasing and will continue to exacerbate the problems.

Throughout its history Kashmir and its valleys and hills and mountains seems to withstand the most radical of changes and present its beauties unfailingly. Kashmir should, ideally, be as neutral as Switzerland. Where religions clash, though, harmony seems impossible.

Geography

There are clearly defined zones throughout the State of Jammu and Kashmir – the Plains, the Foothills, the Pir Panjal mountain range, the Vale of Kashmir – added to which are the distant areas such as the Central Himalayan Zone and the Upper Indus Valley.

The Plains surround Jammu, the winter capital of the State, and are characterised by fan-like alluvial deposits from streams discharging from the foothills. Rainfall is low and occurs mainly as heavy downfalls from June to September when the monsoon winds blow. This countryside is almost entirely denuded of trees. Thorn scrub and grass is the main natural vegetation.

The Foothills rise from 610–2135 m (2000–7000 ft) and are incised and terraced by rivers and by man. More rain falls the higher one goes so that the scrubland gradually gives way to pine forests.

The Pir Panjal Range consists of the first mountain rampart within the Himalayas. There is much winter snow as well as summer rain, a consequence of which is that the area has extensive pasture above the tree line. These pastures are used for summer grazing and for cultivation.

The Vale of Kashmir is a deep basin lying between the Pir Panjal Range and the Central Himalayas with an average altitude of 1615 m (5300 ft). Mineral sediments deposited by the Jhelum river and numerous streams make the waters of Lake Dal and other water stretches very fertile. In summer the monsoon occurs with strong winds and some rain. Up to 2135 m (7000 ft) grow species such as the deodar, the blue pine, walnut, elm and poplar; above 3660 m (12,000 ft) there are meadows of dwarf willow, honeysuckle and rhododendrons growing amidst superb scenery.

The Upper Indus Valley contains the great mountain called Nanga Parbat, the sight of which fascinates most visitors and is best seen from the many walks around Gulmarg.

A visitor to Kashmir will pass through or see something of these differing areas, the most popular being, naturally, the Vale of Kashmir, an area especially proficient in catering for the needs of travellers.

The actual Valley is a large flat declivity some 134 km (84 miles) long and up to 40 km (25 miles) wide. To the north towers the mighty Nanga Parbat, 8114 m (26,620 ft) high, its peak perpetually covered with snow. Other mountain peaks in the vicinity but not visible from the Valley are K2, or Mount Godwin Austen, 8620 m (28,278 ft), and Mount Angram, high in the Hindu Kush, 7750 m (25,426 ft).

The river Jhelum flows from beyond Anantanagar at the southern end of the Valley, through the Vale and the northern Lake Wular, around the Pir Panjal mountains, along the Pakistan border past Rawalpindi to the city of Jhelum. From here it is swelled by many tributaries until it eventually joins the Indus whose estuary is to the south of Karachi.

When visibility is clear the flight from New Delhi over the foothills and into the mountains, eventually sighting the Kashmir Valley, is both awe-inspiring and exhilarating.

Population and language

The population of Jammu and Kashmir is approaching 6 million, the majority of whom are Muslims. The main languages spoken are Kashmiri

Snow peaks at Gulmarg

and Dogri, added to which are others such as Urdu, Batti, Pahari, Punjabi, Dadri, Gujiri, Ladakhi and Hindi. Dogri is the language of the Dogras, the erstwhile rulers of Kashmir.

It is as well to remember that the whole of the State of Jammu and Kashmir is a sensitive region and some parts are strictly out of bounds. Adventurous trekkers are advised to stick to the guided routes at all times. For travel beyond the immediate surroundings of the Kashmir Valley, for shooting or fishing for instance, necessary permits must be obtained.

2 Religion

Islam

The foremost religion in Kashmir is that of Islam, in various writings referred to as Mohammedism, Moslem or Muslim or, in some rare cases, Mussulman. All names mean the same thing and are used to indicate a mainstream of Islamic religious thinking.

In order not to confuse the religion of the Muslims with the more fundamental Islamisation beliefs now being imposed throughout many areas of the Gulf, I have chosen to refer here to Mohammedism as the religion of the majority of the people of Jammu and Kashmir. This religion is divided into two main sub-groups, one called Shi'ite and the other Sunni, and there is inherent conflict between the two groups.

The founder of the Islamic religion was the Prophet Mohammed, hence the name Mohammedism. Mohammed was born at Mecca, in what is now Saudi Arabia, in AD 570, of a family of the Quaraish tribe. The child was something of a marvel. Being orphaned when only six years old, his grandfather took over his care and when he was twelve took him on a journey to Syria. The story goes, and there is no reason to disbelieve it, that half way there, on staying with a Christian monk named Bahira, the monk exclaimed that there was a 'cloud following you and it has stopped over your caravan'. The monk then examined the body of Mohammed and discovered the mark of prophethood between the boy's shoulder blades. The monk counselled immediate return to Mecca, fearing that harm might come to Mohammed, advice upon which his grandfather acted.

From the time of his return to Mecca, Mohammed's reputation for being trustworthy, honest and wise increased. Some time afterwards he did go to Syria, this time at the behest of a wealthy merchant's widow called Khadija. She said that if he would take care of her goods she would pay him more liberally than had others, and he returned successful, having made much profit for the widow. She was so delighted that she sent Mohammed a proposal of marriage. He accepted and they were, indeed, married, he being 25 and she 40 years old.

More and more his spiritual nature necessitated his going alone into the desert to meditate. It was on one of these lonely occasions that the Angel Gabriel spoke to him about a new religion and bade him write down his message which came directly from God. The first revelation happened when Mohammed was 40 years old, in AD 610. Later, the *Qur'an*, or *Koran* as it is known in the West, was gradually revealed to him in simple sentences or paragraphs, from which he began to teach the new religion.

Mohammed was recognised as a prophet and he preached the beginnings of a faith which was to become all-powerful throughout Asia. He died, aged 62, in Medina, the city after Mecca that is most sacred to the Muslims.

A Muslim must believe in one God, in good and evil, and in fate and a life after death. The Muslim faith, then full of zeal and awareness, was more than a religion which people could follow; it called upon them to spread the word, by force if necessary, and many were those who accepted the Islamic way rather than die. Mohammedism's spread throughout the West was checked by Christianity (with which, oddly, it has much in common) in mid-France. Eastwards its influence waxed so strong that eventually Mohammedan dhows invaded India via the Indus; it was then AD 711.

There are no actual priests in Mohammedism but in practice each mosque will be found to have in charge of it a Mullah – a fairly powerful figure in the community, as witnessed in present-day Iran. Everyone is his own priest in charge of his own spirituality, and this makes fanaticism never far below the surface. Mohammedans believe that each person is responsible for his own actions and will answer for them on the Day of Judgement. The whole life is, or should be, dedicated to the worship of God. Compulsory duties are to say prayers five times a day, to give alms, to fast in the month of Ramadan and to make a pilgrimage to Mecca once during a lifetime. Before prayers the hands must be washed with pure water up to the wrists three times, the mouth and the nose must be cleansed by rinsing, as must both arms up to the elbows; finally the feet must be washed three times. It is not surprising, therefore, that one sees water pools and running taps adjacent to all mosques. After such ablutions, the faithful can worship according to the tenets of the holy *Koran*. The *Koran* contains 114 chapters which themselves contain 6200 verses, and there is no doubt as to its historical authenticity. Mohammed appointed learned writers to set down exactly the revelations he received.

Mohammedans believe that to worship God through images such as idols or any representation of the human form is blasphemous. It is this belief more than any other that brought about the desecration of most Hindu architecture during Muslim rule over India.

Muslim tomb of Akbar at Sikander

The Islamic calendar is based on the lunar system and the months determined by the appearance of the new moon. This dating began after Mohammed had moved from Mecca to Medina, 482 km (300 miles) distant. The year 1988, therefore, in the Islamic calendar, would be 1408 AH – After Hiraj – the name given to Mohammed's migration to Medina.

There are four great religious occasions in the Islamic year. The most well-known to Westerners is Muharram, which happens during February. The festival remembers Hussain, Mohammed's grandson, the son of Ali by Fatima, who was the daughter of Mohammed. A period of fasting is followed by a procession in which each community of Muslims in an area carries a representation of the tomb of Hussain. These are called 'tazia' and are several feet high, made of a light wooden construction which is covered in tissue paper and tinsel and coloured stripes in the form of a domed and minaretted building, much like a small Taj Mahal. The 'tazias' are taken to the most convenient water, either river or lake, and are immersed to prayers and chanting. Fervour runs high at this time and it takes only a small incident to spark off trouble.

The festival of Bakr Id, in January, is in memory of Abrahim offering to sacrifice his son, Ishmael – a story related in the *Koran*. On this occasion goats or other animals are sacrificed.

Ramadan, October time, is the month-long festival when continuous daily fasting is observed. Neither food nor drink may be taken between sunrise and sunset. Because of the lunar calendar it is a movable feast. At the end of Ramadan there is the festival called Id-ul-Fitr, when fasting is over and feasting begins.

These festivals are very much a part of the Kashmiri way of life and are extremely interesting to observe. The most convenient of them is Ramadan, around October when Kashmir is aglow with autumn, turning the colour of the famous Chennar trees from green through yellow to a burning red.

Hinduism

Hinduism was not founded by any one sage or teacher in the way that, for instance, Christianity was founded by Jesus Christ, or Islam by the Prophet Mohammed, neither was it planned in the socio-political sense as a means of public control or order. It grew out of the ancient Vedic scriptures, interpreted by an early intellectual named Manu. He translated the meanings of Vedism (the worship of nature) into a domestic code that would be understood by the people, and he created four principal castes in Hindu society. This division of the populace proved to be a religious and social control that has lasted throughout the years. From these divisions sprang the way of life that is loosely called Hinduism. The legends are so interwoven throughout a Hindu's life that they have become fact and are now very real beliefs.

Over 80 per cent of India's population is Hindu; the reverse is so, though, in Kashmir, where one might say that over 80 per cent are Muslim. A Hindu believes in one God, but through many manifestations. It may be through Lord Krishna, or Lord Siva, or Lord Vishnu, or be a

Hindu gods – facade of Meenakshi Temple, Madurai

mixture of all the vast pantheon of gods, of which there are many thousands. In the temples will be found deities represented in the form of the many mythological characters in the great Hindu epics such as the *Mahabharata* (this is the longest poem ever written, containing over three million words). The heart of the *Mahabharata* is the *Bhagavad Gita*, or Sacred Song. There are, too, the *Upanishads*; the Sanskrit verses called the *Puranas*; and the marvellous story of the *Ramayana*. It is within these writings that the beliefs of Hinduism can be found.

Hinduism is based on the idea that each individual will go through a progression of rebirths that eventually lead to a spiritual salvation which frees him from this cycle and leads to Nirvanah. Bad actions in life can lead to a lower reincarnation and, conversely, good actions to a higher reincarnation. The way a person behaves in life is called Karma. Karma, therefore, is self-controlled. The other daily factor of Hinduism, Dharma, is the inevitable by which man is controlled, i.e. by natural laws, by the universe, by his caste, which is irrevocable, and by a moral code that is inherent. A Hindu practices three basics, puja (worship), the burning of the dead and the observance of caste. The Hindu does not proselytize, as do the Christians and the Muslims, and no one not born a Hindu can become one.

The principal caste in Hinduism, the highest, is the Brahmin or priest caste, followed by the Kshastrias, the warriors, fighters or governors. Then come the Vaisyas, the farmers, craftsmen and traders and after them the Sudras, who do manual or physical work such as labouring. The people who have no caste were once called Untouchables; now, though, they are referred to as Harijans, or Children of God, as Mahatma Gandhi called them, and they do all the menial and dirty work.

The caste system has not changed since Independence. After thousands of years it will take much longer to eradicate this social separating and one questions whether or not Hindu society could survive without caste. (Unlike the rest of India, in Kashmir there is little to be observed of caste, but it exists.)

The principal deities of Hinduism are:

Brahma, the creator. He has four heads from which sprang the Vedas, the early scriptures. He is considered to be the God of wisdom.

Saraswati, Brahma's wife. She is depicted riding on a swan and is the goddess of learning.

Siva, is worshipped in the form of a lingam, a phallic symbol, most frequently found in a Siva temple. He is known as the destroyer.

Parvati, Siva's wife, the interceder.

Nandi, the bull. The bull was Siva's mount and is always seen in a Sivite temple.

Ganesh, the elephant-headed son of Siva. He is thought to bring good luck and is often worshipped before undertaking new enterprises.

Vishnu, the preserver. The second most important Hindu god, he appears incarnated as Krishna and as Rama, the hero of the epic *Ramayana*. Krishna is the god of love. His childhood, adolescence and manhood are recounted in the *Bhagavad Gita*.

Lakshmi, the wife of Vishnu. Often depicted seated on a lotus, she represents wealth and prosperity and is represented in one incarnation as Sita, the wife of Rama.

These deities, in one manifestation or another, will be found throughout India in temples, on civic architecture, on wayside shrines, on the summit of any high ground, in the home, on the classical stage in the form of dance and song and, by no means least, in modern India and, therefore in Kashmir, on the cinema screen.

Hinduism is, therefore, a way of life, bound by ancient beliefs in mythology, and it contains the tenets by which the Hindu lives, the disciplines that organise his family life, his feelings about nature, about sexuality, about birth and death, and about life after death. It is a wholeness that satisfies the masses individually; it has no dogma and no rule for all. It is a very personal religion and to those who are not Hindu presents an attractive pattern for a spiritual life.

Sikhism

Guru Nanak, the founder of the Sikh religion, was born in 1469. He was a member of the caste known as Kshastrias – those who, according to the Laws of Manu, were allowed to learn the Vedas but could not become a religious leader, teacher or priest; they were of the fighting or warrior caste. The caste system had become inflexible and oppressive by the fifteenth century; from cradle to the grave one was compelled to live within one's caste. Guru Nanak was not alone in opposing the caste system, but he was powerful enough as a personality actually to become a religious teacher; and he rejected the Vedas. He taught in the local dialects of the people and accepted disciples from amongst them irrespective of caste. He insisted that all should eat from the same dish, a revolutionary step then and rejected even now by the strict Brahmins.

Guru Nanak was born at Talwandi, a medium-sized village some 64 km (40 miles) south-west of Lahore, now in Pakistan. Throughout his life he tried to unite the Hindu and the Muslim together with all the many other religions then practised in India, so that they would at least understand their differences. For 20 years he travelled with a Muslim poet, Mardana, as his companion as far as Ceylon and Tibet and to Mecca. Through the poet he conveyed his message to the peoples wherever he travelled.

He died in 1539 and tradition records that, as the news spread that he was likely to die, Hindus and Muslims came for a last sight of the great man and there arose a dispute between them, the Hindu saying that he would cremate the Guru's body and the Muslim saying that he would bury it in accordance with Muslim custom. The dispute was eventually ended by the Guru himself. He told the Hindus to place flowers on his right and the Muslims to place flowers on his left, and whichever flowers were fresh on the following day, that side should dispose of his body according to

Sikh Golden Temple, Amritsar

its custom. Then the Guru covered his body with a sheet and he went to sleep. The following morning when the cover was removed both the right and the left flowers were fresh, but the body of Guru Nanak had gone!

This story, fact or fiction, points to the Guru's constant teaching – that there is no difference between a Hindu and a Muslim, then the main differing groups, and that God was the same whatever the method of worship.

The Sikhs continued in the steps of their first Guru for centuries, adding to the prayers and songs – hymns really – until all these rules and praise and worship were gathered into one volume. This has now become the scripture for all Sikhs and is called the *Guru Granth Sahib*.

The golden age of Sikhism was under the reign of Maharaja Ranjit Singh. He employed both Hindu and Muslim in his armies which he organised on Western lines, with many Europeans among their officers, and for little over 40 years the Punjab became home, a real homeland for the Sikhs.

At the time of Independence there were many Sikhs who hoped that the British Government would create a separate state in the Punjab. This was not to be and still today there are agitators among the more militant Sikhs who continue to press this cause.

The Sikhs have a reputation for being volatile, war-like and hot-tempered; their first Guru was a Kshastria, one born into the fighting caste, so perhaps this is not to be wondered at. Most of the Sikh men seem to be incredibly tall and all but the most modern wear a turban. Though this is not mandatory, there are some things that are and they are referred to as the five 'K's': the kesh, the kangha, the kirpan, the kachs and the kara. The kesh is the long uncut hair which distinguishes the Sikh and is the first rule to be obeyed. To keep this uncut hair tidy he uses a comb, or kangha. The kirpan is a sword that can be anything up to 90 cm (3 ft) in length. These days, because of the various laws that forbid the carrying of offensive weapons, this frequently takes the form of a piece of metal embedded in the comb, or kangha. The kachs are short cotton trousers worn under long trousers, as underpants. When fighting, these short trousers were more practical than the dhoti, the loin cloth. The kara is a steel bracelet worn on the right wrist and, together with the turban, is the most noticeable symbol of the Sikh. In twentieth-century India though, with fashion being so important to the young, not everyone wearing a steel bracelet will be a Sikh, just as not all people with the surname Singh will be a Sikh; but all Sikhs have the name Singh! Singh means lion.

Sikhism could be described as the result of the efforts of a protestor against the old laws which, through preaching and example and discipleship, have led from a movement to a religion, a religion that has its scripture, its initiation rites, its rites of marriage and death and its places of pilgrimage.

The true Sikhs practise tolerance and love for all (sometimes difficult to believe when one sees them in war-like mood pressing for the creation of a separate State) and in their Gurdwaras, their temples, they will welcome anyone and offer shelter and food and allow them to rest for a while.

Buddhism

Buddhism was once the established religion of the Kashmir region and still is the main religion of the northern area called Ladakh, once a part of Tibet.

It is generally accepted that Buddha was born in 624 BC and died in 544 BC. The Buddha's name was Siddharta Gautama, two names often used as first names for sons today in many Hindu families. It is even considered suitable as the name of an hotel! Gautama changed his name to that of Buddha after receiving enlightenment from God – Buddha meaning 'The Enlightened One'.

After renouncing all worldly pleasures and all personal possessions he left his home and his wife, whom he had married at the age of 16, and, with his hair cut off, and poorly dressed, he joined two holy men. He was then 29 years old. The two men were Brahmin priests and he wished to observe their holy life and practise their austerities. The rigours of this new life were heightened by the fact that he came from a wealthy family and was used to all the comfort and privilege that that brings. He was tormented by memories of the indulgent living of others whilst so many had so little, and was determined to find a means of relieving the suffering of the less privileged.

At the age of 35, when sitting under a Bo tree on the banks of the river Niranjara near Gaya, in the present-day State called Bihar, enlightenment came to him from God and his future at once became clear.

He became known as Buddha and immediately began to preach his way of life – the way that had been revealed to him when meditating. He preached his first sermon at Sarnath, 6 km (4 miles) from Varanasi (Benares), telling his listeners stories and parables in the same way as did Jesus Christ, and he soon attracted a large following.

He called the way of life 'The Middle Way', a kind of centre course between the asceticism as practised in the monastery and the indulgent uncontrolled life of the affluent, and he soon attracted a group of disciples around him. There were no social differences, all men were (and are) equal on becoming a member of the Buddhist faith; one automatically sheds material values, or lack of them, and becomes only a follower of Buddha.

The Buddha died at the venerable old age of 80 and attained Nirvanah, the freeing of the soul from the cycles of rebirth. After the cremation of his body its remains were divided amongst several of his followers and each part was enshrined in a 'stupa', a domed memorial mound.

In India Buddhism developed swiftly, largely encouraged by the Emperor Ashoka who had embraced the Buddha's teachings. Ashoka's empire extended everywhere except in the south of India. In the north the spread of Buddhism was assured. Ashoka erected huge pillars of stone wherever he went and had written on them the virtues of Buddhism. These 'edicts' of Ashoka were his personal law which was based upon the teachings of Buddha. One such pillar is at Sarnath. On the top of this pillar once stood the four-headed lion that is now the national symbol of India.

Buddhism is important in India if for no other reason than that it was conceived there. (The other religions founded in India are Hinduism, Jainism and, much later, Sikhism.) There are about 5 million Buddhists in India, an oddly small number when compared with the total population of nearly 800 million.

Statue of Lord Buddha, Bodh Gaya

The majority of Buddhists live around the Himalayan region and perhaps the harsh life of the mountain people, which needs fortitude and resourcefulness, makes more natural and easy the following of a religion demanding such a degree of self-discipline, much of which must be provoked by nature, the elements and the isolation.

3 The mountains and the people

The Himalayas

Himalaya is a Sanskrit word which roughly means 'Abode of Snow' or Snowland. The Himalayan Range stretches west to east from the Indus to the Bramaputra and varies in breadth from 96–320 km (60–200 miles). The average height between these two points is 5486 m (18,000 ft), the whole interspersed by gigantic gorges, expansive glaciers and scree slopes of ice and mountain detritus. Some gorges run at a mean level of 915 m (3000 ft) right up to the foot of the snow-capped heights, and, because of this, in some areas the climate can be hot and fertile.

The Western Himalayas are those in which the fabled Vale of Kashmir lies, south of Gilgit and north of the plain of Jammu. To the north is the great mountain range called Karakoram, which means, in Turkish, 'Black Rock Mountain', and which is the highest group of mountains in the world, containing the mighty K2 or Mount Godwin Austen. This mountain range has thirty peaks which rise to over 7315 m (24,000 ft) and is crossed by incredibly, and sometimes fatally, difficult passes.

The foothills of the Himalayas rise from the plains to between 610–2133 m (2000–7000 ft). This steady rise buttresses the great Pir Panjal Range, high above which are meadows warmed in the rarified atmosphere so that they support lush meadows and are often astonishing for their variety of flowers and flowering trees.

Transhumance is a way of life here, and the shepherds migrate to the high altitudes once spring is well under way. They lead their flocks to higher pastures and grazing grounds, those upon which the Pashmina goats are reared. Many goats are wild and survive the harsh elements, giving a thicker and more warm fleece from which the famous Pashmina shawls are woven.

Among the foothills are settlements of a mixture of peoples – Punjabis, Dogri, Tribal and Muslim – all of whom use townships such as Jammu and Srinagar as their main trading centres.

Higher and beyond the Vale of Kashmir, which is hidden amongst these mountains, are those hills leading to Leh, Ladakh and Zanskar. This area is often referred to as 'Little Tibet'. The language here is Ladakhi – of Tibetan origin – and the faith is Buddhist.

The whole of the Himalayan mountain range has been a meeting ground for two major cultures, the Aryans and the Mongolians. These ethnically different people have mixed and merged through time, cultivating the arid region of Ladakh and penetrating through into the lush valley of Kashmir.

Srinagar and its bazaars provides a meeting-place for all the peoples of the mountain region. At some time or another each will make a trek to the city and sell or buy or barter. The shops and markets, emporiums and ancient gullies of the old city of Srinagar contain almost every type of hill person, trading or taking a 'local holiday'. Turbans, shawls, voluminous gowns, burquahs and yashmaks are sold by a whole jumble of people whose lives have been, and are, controlled directly by the mountains that surround them so forbiddingly.

Owing to the voluminous costumes so often worn by Kashmiris and hill people one seldom sees their vigorous bodies, unlike, for instance, at another hill area, Mussoorie, where the Garhwalis shift loads on their back supported by limbs of knotted muscle. The Kashmiri hides his strength with baggy trousers and flowing kaftan or shirt, often cuffed at wrist and ankle. It is a graceful and modest dress in keeping with Mohammedism. The women-folk, too, wear full garments, flowing wool or cotton dresses, often of a drab colour heightened only by a gay headscarf or, perhaps, a mauve or maroon shawl. Around the bazaars the hill people will be seen in their 'best dress' for visiting the 'big city'. Only around their hill settlements will you see evidence of the strength of limbs. (There are some exceptions in that servants around houseboats will be seen stripped to the waist, or bathing in the lake waters. This is largely the influence of European visitors and is not characteristic of the region.)

The mountains and their peoples make the majority of the populace of the Kashmir region so that, whatever one reads about its present, all should be related to its past and its incredibly difficult, defensive and dauntingly-positioned geography.

The character of the Kashmiri

Visitors to Kashmir frequently relate, on returning home, accounts of how, in one way or another, they have been upset by the Kashmiri peoples' eagerness to sell. Tales will be told of being charged too much or exploited by unscrupulous houseboat owners or about having been beleaguered by all manner of persistent traders.

Much of this dissatisfaction or disenchantment stems from the traveller not troubling to understand the way of the people, the way they behave and react to each other – let alone to foreigners – and to endeavour to find out what has contributed to the Kashmiris' thinking processes and life style in order to have moulded them as they now present themselves.

Travellers who do not read about where they are journeying to before setting out should not start their journey, or at least if they do, then complain silently. It is especially needful to read as much as possible about so distant a place as Kashmir and to try to understand something about places and peoples who are so disparate.

If one thinks about Kashmir, set amongst its great mountain ranges, together with its turbulent history, one will see that its peoples have always been dominated by survival either of the elements or the excesses of one ruler or another. Wars for possession of the 'jewel among the mountains' have caused the indigenous population of Kashmiris to ebb and flow on a tide of constant oligarchic change. Muslim, Hindu, Sikh, Rajput – all have had a harsh hand in making survival difficult for the Kashmiri.

It is no surprise, therefore, to find them described as 'devious, shady, tricky, false-tongued, faint-hearted, greedy' – the list is long, by those who write glib articles. A turbulent local history of unscrupulous rulers, some fanatics, some dissolute, most avaricious and all giving no advancement to their conquered peoples, above slavery, is one aspect of character moulding.

Another is Kashmir's history of natural disasters. Throughout each successive age since records began the Valley has been torn apart by earthquakes, avalanches and floods, some of which have wiped out whole sections of the community. One thinks only of the first recorded earthquake during the reign of Sirdar Sena (2082–2041 BC) when water from the surrounding mountains submerged the whole existing city which is now where the huge Lake Wular spreads. One after another, through the years, are chronicled the natural disasters which, added to the frequent heavy snows, destroyed crops and houses and livelihoods; and, as if this were not enough, famine and cholera added to the Kashmiris' tribulations.

Survival was the one constant in the changing pattern of the Kashmiri people. To survive calamity, and conquest, they needed to develop a certain amount of guile, cunning and ruthlessness in both business and barter. Perhaps because of this many succumbed to an increasing lack of personal inner strength, or morality. What did it matter though, when tomorrow might never come? And indeed, for many it did not.

The Kashmiri is a product of his background. Cut off by mountains from other races, cultures, ideas and influences, he has developed his own

A Kashmiri belle

Earthenware seller, Srinagar

characteristics and not even in this present-day relatively easy time, of tourism and money making, can he shed his innate time-burnished traits.

One should try to accept with understanding the calculated intimidation, the guile and the often double standards and realise that it is an integral ingredient of a visit to Kashmir, more especially if you are roughing it as a back-pack traveller, as you will be living much nearer to these annoyances than would those whose visit is cushioned by five star attention.

4 Travel and climate

Formalities

To reach Kashmir it is necessary to go through India. One cannot fly there direct, other than by changing planes at New Delhi from the International Arrival Terminus to the Domestic, and waiting until the next flight for Srinagar is due for take-off. Also, most travellers making the long journey to Kashmir would more than likely wish to see something of India, especially the surroundings of New Delhi and, perhaps, nearby Agra, with the Taj Mahal, and Jaipur. Included, therefore, are some general facts helpful for travel wherever in India may be visited, not forgetting that Kashmir is a part of India and much of the information applies in the State of Jammu and Kashmir.

Tourist Introduction Card and liquor permit
On visiting India a Tourist Introduction Card can be very useful and is easily and freely available from any Tourist Office, usually somewhere at the point of entry into the country. At the same time a liquor permit can be obtained.

The Tourist Information Card will introduce the traveller to government authorities and departments from which assistance may be sought. The liquor permit is required in 'dry' States, such as Gujarat and Tamil Nadu. For the visitor there is no shortage of good Indian spirits, but if imported liquor is desired, then the price will be high.

Visa requirements
A visa is necessary in order to enter India. An application form can be obtained from the Visa Department, India House, Aldwych, London, or from the company responsible for a tour. Any personal application will take time and this must be allowed for if either applying in person or by sending an application form together with the exact amount payable, by crossed postal order, not cheques etc, and the passport, plus three passport

sized photographs. Normally the passport and visa will be returned within two weeks, but there are popular times, such as January and February, when the time taken may be slightly longer. It is better to allow plenty of time when applying as the visa's commencement does not start until arrival in India. The customary length of time allowed on a tourist visa is 90 days. For missionaries and other workers, and nationals of Pakistan and Bangladesh, it will be necessary to obtain separate forms.

Income tax clearance certificate
If your stay in India does not exceed 90 days you are free to leave without this certificate. If your stay is for more than 90 days, you will require this certificate which can be obtained from a local Income Tax Office at the point of departure. Be advised, though, that the process of obtaining one may take the whole day, battling with bureaucracy. If you are lucky you could be in and out of the office within half an hour.

It must be noted that neither a return half of an air ticket nor a new single or return ticket can be used or booked without this certificate in the case of a stay of more than 90 days.

Foreign travel tax
On departing from India there is a tax charged of 100 rupees per person, and travellers are well advised to keep this amount aside from other expenses so that on arrival at the airport the money is available. You will not be allowed to leave the country without paying and, as departure times can be disconcertingly late at night or early in the morning, facilities are not always open for changing travellers cheques. The present foreign travel tax is high compared with not so long ago when it was 20 rupees. Now, after a visit to India, a family of four will be expected to pay the equivalent of £25 (1987). If multiplied by the thousands who depart from India each year it will be seen that there is revenue from this charge running into millions of rupees.

Health regulations

No special inoculations are needed on entering India and travelling up into the State of Jammu and Kashmir, if arriving from the United Kingdom. It is wise, though, to consult the Indian Tourist Department before leaving any country, making sure that enough time is allowed for any necessary treatment, as there may be a change in regulations.

An injection of gamma globulin as a help towards avoiding infectious hepatitis is advisable. This is painless and produces no side-effects and will be given by your doctor. Should any outbreaks of cholera or small-pox occur whilst you are in India, it is a simple thing to get innoculated on the spot. A valid certificate of vaccination against yellow fever is required of all persons entering India from an infected area, otherwise a period of quarantine must be accepted. A list of infected areas is available from the Indian High Commission. The vaccine must have been approved by the World Health Organisation and must have been administered at least ten days before arrival in India.

NB   As Government Health Regulations frequently change, it is a good idea to check with your local health authority on innoculations which, as a safety measure, may be currently recommended.

Indian currency

Based on the rupee, it is divided into paises, of which there are 100 to a rupee. It is well to remember that an Indian will think in paises and not in rupees. Contrary to what the affluent will relate, there are very many everyday items that cost less than a rupee. This applies as much to Kashmir as to other parts of India. For the speedy tourist, though, for whom the currency is strange, it is simpler to think in rupees.

Indian Standard Time

Time in India is $5\frac{1}{2}$ hours ahead of G.M.T. and $4\frac{1}{2}$ hours ahead of Central European Time. It is $11\frac{1}{2}$ hours ahead of the United States.

Routes to Kashmir

Via Indian Airlines
During the tourist season there are daily flights direct from New Delhi. The flying distance is approx 773 km (480 miles) and for flying time just over two hours. There are also flights which go from New Delhi via Amritsar and Jammu or via Chandigarh, Amritsar and Jammu, and by stopping and starting you do get a chance to see more of the scenery and have stop-overs if desired. If not stopping-over, this circuitous journey will take over six hours. After arriving at Srinagar and going through the formalities the journey into the centre of the city will take about 20 minutes by taxi, longer by bus.

Via Indian Railways
After arriving at Jammu one either takes a bus, hires a car, or shares a taxi, agreeing the price beforehand. The drive on to Srinagar will take about

Indian highway scene

eight hours depending on road conditions; it could take twelve hours. The scenery is superb over the famous Banihal Pass which rises as high as 2286 m (7500 ft) above sea level. It is not possible to go all the way to Srinagar via rail, one has to end this part of the journey at Jammu and travel by alternative transport. There is a railway service from Bombay direct and from Calcutta. Not all carriages are equipped with air-conditioning and the long journey in the summertime can be hot and tedious, even in first class ordinary non-airconditioned.

The railways

The Indian railway system is the second largest railway in the world and the largest in Asia. The State railways were nationalised by the Indian Government in April 1950, since when both indigenous and tourist traffic

Typical Indian railway station

have greatly increased. It must be remembered that millions of Indians travel within India daily, both for work and as tourists in their own country. Seats are at a premium and booking ahead is essential if making arrangements other than via a tour operator.

Concessional fares are available on most routes, such as the hill station journeys, with circular tickets for a good period depending on the time chosen by the traveller; it may be for seven days or for ninety days. It should be noted that an Indrail pass does *not* guarantee a seat on any train whatever the class. Reservations and bookings should be made in the ordinary way at the railway station or through an Indian Agent, using the Indrail pass only to fulfil the requirements for cheaper travel.

Often visitors wishing to see Kashmir will combine this with seeing another part of India, the most convenient, using the railways, being going to Agra to see the Taj Mahal and up into Rajasthan to Jaipur where there are many attractions. A week should be allowed for this, or indeed any other itinerary that is combined with Kashmir.

Sleeping accommodation on Indian trains must always be reserved in advance and a reservation ticket extra to the journey ticket obtained. On arrival at the station your name will be found posted on a passenger list, much like the old passenger ships' lists, and one should check both the number of the bogey (carriage) and the compartment number in that bogey; the porters, called 'coolies', will be carrying your bags and will know the correct place on the platform at which to wait if the train is not in the station. If it is waiting he will know where to take you.

The actual sleeping arrangements can be either a coupé (a compartment for two) or a compartment for four. The coupé is usually given to a married couple or to two single women travelling together. Some of the older rolling stock still has the coupé with the attached bathroom, otherwise all recent bogeys have this facility at each end. One of them will be with Eastern plumbing, (i.e. squat-type lavatory) and the other will be the conventional Western type. There will be a shower in the roof, not always immediately seen, but it is there and will be painted 'railway green', a pale grey-green that spreads throughout all Indian trains from the corridors to the rexine seating. Beware of the shower, though, for if it is used during the summer time days the water may scald you, being solar-heated (the water tanks are on the roof of the train!).

If bedding is needed, and it may very much be needed on an overnight journey up to Jammu as the nights can become quite cold, then it can be obtained by reserving it in advance and obtaining another ticket or chitty. Bedding is called a 'bed-roll', which is a rolled up collection of pillow, pillow-case, sheet, blanket and towel, all scrupulously clean. The bogey attendant will bring it to you and, when the time comes for sleep, will return and make it up for you. In the morning he will come again and check each item and take it away. The charge for this is 5 rupees, about 20p.

Porterage is always available at stations and airports and bus stands. At the railway stations the coolies wear red shirts and coats and a red turban which they wind round their heads as a sweat band. They will have, or should have, an arm band around their upper arm to which is fixed a brass number plate on which is written their registration number.

In Indian economics there is a rate for most jobs, and foreign travellers, either in innocence or ignorance, upset this by giving rupees away too generously because to them it seems very little money. To an Indian one rupee represents 100 paises. The sensible way to travel in any country is by observing the economics that prevail and trying to stick to them.

Railway travel is a marvellous way of seeing India, and the comfort of a first class non-airconditioned booking, though not decoratively attractive in the Western sense, is nevertheless adequate. Meals can be had as well as non-alcoholic drinks and fruit and there is also a small library on some trains. To travel first class air-conditioned is really to travel in style, but it doubles the cost of ordinary first class, and, for the money, many would rather fly.

Srinagar is 880 km (546 miles) from New Delhi and there are roughly four main train services daily. The journey takes over 13 hours and some of this time will be spent over-night. There are Tourist Reception Offices at all main line railway stations that will render any assistance needed. Trains operating up to Jammu have interesting names, such as the Jammu

Mail, the DN Super Fast, the Sealdah Express, the Shalimar Express. One should try and book on a train that arrives at Jammu by mid-day the next day, thus allowing plenty of time to make further arrangements to go straight up to Srinagar or to stay for a while at Jammu.

The seasons in Kashmir

The spring season of March and April is one of the most beautiful around the Vale of Kashmir and among the hills, with the blooming of meadow flowers, iris and new leaves, and the trees laden with blossom. The nights, however, will be cold, as will most of the days, and cold winds blow frequently. In May and June the weather is more settled and this is one of the best times to visit Kashmir. After June and to the end of August it can be disconcertingly hot. Mosquitoes are whining around and the centre of the lake seems the only way to keep comparatively cool and, perhaps, escape being bitten.

The end of August sees the Vale very full indeed. Indian tourists come in their droves. Houseboats are crowded, the lake waters are churned up with water skiing. The shops will be full and, for the Kashmiri traders, it is like an extended harvest festival. The money rolls in and the traders grin and prepare for the long winter ahead, when no one visits Srinagar. A Kashmiri who does not have a city outlet for selling his goods, somewhere south of his State, has to make enough money to keep him and his family for the seven months when the Valley is cut off for some of the time.

Before this, though, there is the autumn season when, by October, the leaves on the chenar trees will be starting to turn gold and the fantastic red that seems to set fire to the surrounding hills and Moghul Gardens. The saffron plants do not bloom until November so that few visitors are around to see this glorious sight. The snows fall from November onwards and will cover the Valley and the southern areas around Jammu with a deep layer of snow that will last until the first thaws the following February.

The monsoon breaks in July and August but the Vale of Kashmir is protected from all but the most fierce rains by the Pir Panjal range of mountains. There are, however, frequent thunder storms, but they pass quickly and in so doing bring drama to the scenery and produce fantastic sunsets.

Recommended clothing
Spring – medium-weight woollens and warm top coat.
Summer – light cottons, light woollens and a raincoat.
Autumn – light woollens and a raincoat or jacket.
Winter – heavy woollens and a thick overcoat.

Winter – February at Gulmarg

For trekking, hiking, climbing and skiing it is essential to arrive complete with personal equipment and adequate clothing, plus warm bedding if not staying at a first class hotel or on a houseboat.

Climate

For the area in and around the Vale of Kashmir, which is the most frequented region visited by tourists, this list of expected temperatures will be a guide to enable sensible and appropriate planning for a visit. It will be seen that there is, for instance, a good mean temperature for summer weather and, alternatively, a cold time when winter skiing can be enjoyed. Temperatures are quoted in centigrade and are those issued by the State of Jammu and Kashmir Tourist Information Office.

These temperatures are the average taken over the month. There is a caution inherent, in that even on the hottest days, between June and September, the nights can turn chilly. Not all the nights do turn cold; some remain little different from the day temperatures. These variations are expected in so mountainous a region.

Month	Maximum	Minimum
January	4.4	−2.3
February	7.9	−0.8
March	13.4	3.5
April	19.3	7.4
May	24.6	11.2
June	29.0	14.4
July	30.8	18.4
August	29.9	17.9
September	28.3	12.7
October	22.6	5.7
November	15.5	−0.1
December	8.8	−1.8

Photography

For colour slide photography it is good advice to take with you the best camera you can afford. Conditions in India vary so much, especially in the Vale of Kashmir and among the mountains, that you may need the more sophisticated type of camera, one on which both speed and aperture can be adjusted. For snapshots, an automatic camera will be adequate. Buy your film before you leave for India and Kashmir.

The prevailing sun and the quality of the air are the main factors to be considered. Circumstances can be deceptive, and the more adjustments of which a camera is capable, the better. It is not always a guarantee of good slides or photographs to have an instamatic camera as these often have average correlations that will not take into account such elements as air pollution, refracted sunlight, dust in the atmosphere or, most of all, the angle of the sun. From around 10.30am to 4.30pm the sun will, in the summertime, be overhead, causing strong downward light, and this gives intense glare on horizontal planes and deep shadows on vertical ones. A camera that is capable of manual control will present fewer problems and better results in the end.

In Kashmir one has the daytime problem of refraction owing to surrounding snows, something that should be compensated for before clicking, or be automatically corrected by appropriate filters. Water, too, the great photographic element of the Valley of Kashmir, is constantly fascinating and challenging to the photographer; before 11am and after 4pm are golden rules as mid-day photography can be very disappointing. A permanently fixed ultra-violet filter and a lens hood are desirable.

Tea seller

There are countless developing shops in India and all around the bazaars of Kashmir (Srinagar, for instance) where overnight one can have developed a black and white film complete with postcard-size prints. It is a cheap and speedy service. Colour film processing is not so readily available, the only reliable laboratories for slide processing, or print making, being in New Delhi and Bombay, and the time taken for processing a film might be longer than your stay. It is better to wait and have colour film processed in the West.

Remember to check the expiry date on films before leaving as deterioration accelerates faster in a hot climate.

Buy a security protection bag, usually made of lead foil, in which to keep both used and unused film. All airports have different methods of checking hand baggage and while you will be assured by the operators that X-ray machines and scanners will not harm film, they might. Though the protection bags are not claimed to be fully proof against misadventure, if you use one you will have the satisfaction of knowing that you have taken the precaution. Never put exposed or unexposed film in baggage that will not be accompanying you – this is subjected to security scanners before loading and your film could suffer.

Facilities

Convention complex

The convention-meetings-exhibitions-conferences complex is built by the bank of Lake Dal near to the entrance-way to the Chashmashahi Gardens and provides modern facilities of international standard. The complex has a seating capacity for 400 plus 200 extra in the balcony; the meeting rooms can accommodate 250 people or be converted into a banquet hall for 400 or smaller, as the occasion demands. Many are the Indian weddings that need catering for 400, rather more in fact.

There are other facilities such as reception, lounge and bar, cafeteria and dining room and a swimming pool. There is, too, the useful addition of simultaneous translation resources.

Sports complex

Called the Sheri-i-Kashmir Sports Complex, this is the third largest in the country. It has a capacity for 4050 spectators and has been planned according to international standards. Facilities include tennis, basketball, badminton, table tennis, gymnastics, boxing, archery, an indoor rifle range and weightlifting. There are players' warm-up rooms, lounges for judges, coaches and the press, TV commentator boxes and radio announcer booths. Food of all kinds can be supplied on request and there is a public snack bar.

Shopping centres and markets

For some visitors to Kashmir the time may be short and, therefore, a few addresses for souvenir shopping may be useful. At Government-controlled shops one should not expect to bargain; at others it will be expected that you do.

Government Arts Emporium, Residency Road
Government Central Market, Exhibition Grounds
Shopping Area, Boulevard
Shopping Area, the Bund
Shopping Area, Lal Chowk and Budshah Chowk

Sightseeing

Arrangements can be made at the Tourist Reception Centre, in the centre of Srinagar, for any mode of vehicle for sightseeing from horse-drawn to taxi. The latter will cost the most. There are regular organised bus or coach excursions and a complete list of these, plus the cost, would be most helpful to a visitor if obtained on arrival from the airport or by road at the Tourist Reception Centre.

All methods of transport stop here; it is the great meeting and information place and has the approval and blessing of the Kashmiri Government. One can, for instance, book accommodation here, especially on a houseboat. The staff are really helpful and do all they can to make one welcome and solve all problems. It is what they are there for and use should be made of all the facilities available.

Disregard touts. There will be plenty around telling all sorts of stories and offering all sorts of help, but in the long run it is better to go through the approved Tourist Office.

Complaints

Under the Jammu and Kashmir Registration of Tourist Act, 1978, Officers of the State Tourism Department are vested with special powers for the settlement of complaints. In case of complaint write to the Director of Tourism, Tourist Reception Centre, Srinagar.

5 Health care

Healthy travel

A good start to trouble-free travel in India is not to start with the conviction that you will be ill!

Thousands upon thousands of Indians live their lives suffering only minor illnesses, but, just as anywhere else in the world, there are times when illness does occur and if it happens to you, then there are plenty of well-qualified Indian doctors around.

Do not, therefore, arm yourself with half the contents of a chemist's shop. Take only those medicines that have been prescribed specially by your doctor for any permanent or temporary complaint – blood pressure tablets, for instance, or tablets for a heart condition.

A debilitating and all too common indisposition for a tourist is an upset stomach. For stomach-ache, diarrhoea and vomiting the treatment is easy and swift, safe and sure. It is most likely if you are travelling with a group tour that the tour leader will have a supply of tablets that will alleviate the symptoms. If this is not the case then remedies such as Lomotol, Imodium or Thalazol will be quick and effective and are readily available. For any ailment, beware of drugs containing sulphur as you may be allergic to them and thereby make matters worse.

It is better to let the body itself deal with these matters but on a holiday, time will be precious and such healing may take too long. Take curd and rice and bananas only, with a little sugar and a pinch of salt. Drink plenty of water that has been boiled or that is known to be pure (see below, *Drinking water*).

AIDS

There has been some evidence of this disease in India, often among student communities. The Government of India now requires a certificate of freedom from AIDS of a student who will be spending the usual long time at college or at university. This requirement is, at the time of writing, applicable to students of certain countries, a list of which may be obtained from the local High Commission Office of the Government of India or the Government of India Tourist Office.

As knowledge about AIDS changes rapidly so do restrictions all over the world. It is a very wise precaution, therefore, to enquire about up-to-date procedural requirements before starting one's journey.

At the present time there are no AIDS checks required for tourists.

Malaria
Malaria is to be prevented at all costs and tablets that have been recommended by your doctor should be taken according to the instructions. Daraprim is a good weekly tablet, or pellet, and has no side effects.

Malaria is spread by the mosquito which, before puncturing the skin and sucking the blood, will probably have alighted among filthy conditions. It is important, therefore, to remember to take tablets regularly on the same day of each week. One should start taking them a week before leaving for India and continue after returning for another week. Remember that malaria can be a killer.

Rabies
Rabies is widespread throughout India and animals, even domestic ones such as pet dogs and monkeys, anywhere should be discouraged from getting too close. A dog will slink away if you just pretend to throw a stone at it. Monkeys nearby temples should not be fed. Temples are a favourite place for both monkeys and nut-vendors who will plead with you to feed 'the Holy Monkey' (Hanuman, the Monkey God in the Hindu pantheon of Gods). There will be plenty who will feed them, so let them and stand back and watch.

Polio
It is a wise precaution to ask your doctor for a dose of polio vaccine before leaving for India. If you have had one recently then ask for a booster; it lasts for five years and will prevent what could be a frightful illness.

Infectious hepatitis
Though a gamma globulin injection is not proof against this infection it is a wise precaution and will certainly help protect you, especially for a short stay. Gamma globulin is decreasingly effective over a period of six months. There are no side effects from this injection, which is usually given in the buttocks.

Mosquito bites

Only a few mosquito bites are malarial. The number of varieties in India,
though, seems uncountable and the taking of a suitable prophylactic is
essential. The swelling, accompanied by a red mark of varying intensity,
will last for five days no matter what ointment is applied. Ointment will, at
best, only alleviate the itching. A good anaesthetic cream or gel will ease
the itching and certainly prevent the need to scratch. These bites seem not
to show on Indians, but they get bitten just as much as others.

Prevention is another help. Sleep under a mosquito net where necessary
if the room is not air-conditioned. In Kashmir the windows of houseboats
are protected by fine gauze netting and the houseboat-boy will advise if
mosquito nets are needed. Doors and windows should be kept shut
everywhere in India, between the hours of dawn and nine in the morning,
and again from four to eight in the evening. These are the times when
mosquitoes are most active. Apply one of the proprietary repellants.
Odomos is available all over India; oil of citron is good also, but the most
pleasant is oil of lavender, unavailable in India but obtainable in the
West. Dab on wrists, ankles, neck and on the hair and it will repel all but
the most persistent.

Drinking water

Do not drink water anywhere other than in recognised hotels, the homes of
friends and in municipally safe areas. In these places water will have been
treated by filtration and in some cases will have been boiled. Boiling is
always a good safeguard.

Seritabs, a preparation available in Indian chemist shops, is in the form
of a tablet which renders water absolutely safe for drinking. One tablet
should be put into 3 litres ($5\frac{1}{4}$ pints) of water (the equivalent of four squash
bottles) and left for half an hour by which time the water will be ready for
drinking.

It is essential to drink plenty of water when the climate is hot and humid
as your body will need it and mineral waters, soda water and all the soft
drinks that are available are not a substitute. Tea without milk is a good
alternative; it will also be safe. *Always travel with a supply of your own water;
every Indian will.*

Dehydration can happen insidiously and you may not realise it. It is at
this time that the body's system is most vulnerable. Salt intake is
important, but it comes in sufficient quantities in Indian food. If, however,
you go on a rigorous trek or climb, then you may suffer from a faint feeling
in the legs, as though they are unable to support you. As salt is unpalatable
raw and can be an emetic, salt tablets are available. They release salt into

the system slowly and, after half an hour's rest, such symptoms will have disappeared. A good pick-me-up after dehydration is Electral Powder which contains all the essential minerals and trace elements needed to revive and feed the body, in a palatable form. Perspiring, diarrhoea, vomiting and exertions such as athletics, skiing etc. are causes of dehydration and the orangey drink of Electral Powder replaces lost minerals and overcomes muscle weakness, stiff neck and listlessness.

If you suffer from high blood pressure, then salt tablets must be advised by a doctor; Electral Powder is harmless. See also advice regarding ice on p. 59.

Drinking water in Kashmir

The State Water Board pipes and pumps drinking water to every houseboat. This water has passed the necessary laboratory standards and is quite acceptable for drinking. The houseboat-boy may pass this through a filter before bottling it and putting it in a refrigerator ready for use. If one is still unsure then he will boil it before filtering it; indeed many houseboat owners insist on this rather than have complaints from guests.

Many travellers will be wary of the water no matter what the precautions taken and for them there are readily available an assortment of bottled waters, 'natural waters', in plastic containers. The effervescent mineral waters, such as Vichy, will be obtainable only in the larger hotels.

For those who plan a longish stay in Kashmir it is better to come to terms with the local water and get used to drinking it. It comes from large collection zones of pure melting snows and running streams from high in the mountains, and is then treated by filtration.

In the months of June, July and August, Kashmiri days will be scorchingly hot. Tea, without milk, is the most refreshing drink. The houseboat-boy will make it for you continuously if you desire. Kashmiri tea is different from ordinary tea in that it is made by infusing green tea leaves, cinnamon and cardamon and sugar and is an excellent alternative for quenching a thirst.

Some important tips to remember are:

never drink the lake water
be careful of gulping if swimming
beer is a poor substitute for water
alcohol should only be taken after sundown

Doctors, dentists and chiropodists

Good doctors are available throughout India but medical treatments are not free. It is wise, therefore, to ask the charge for treatment after consultation so that you are prepared for the account. The charge will include the initial consultation.

Teeth should be checked before leaving for India but if treatment becomes necessary a doctor or the hotel reception will put a visitor in touch with a dentist who will be acceptable to a Westerner.

Foot care can be obtained only in the large cities but even there chiropody is not common. The Indians' feet seem to be indestructable! From an early age Indians of all classes are accustomed to walking barefoot at some time or another of the day; indeed for most it is more comfortable than wearing sandals.

Walking barefoot, especially around religious buildings, can cause all manner of foot ailments, the most frequent and lasting being athlete's foot. Always wear a pair of socks, they are acceptable to both temple and mosque and serve two purposes: they protect against disease and they protect against the heat of the sun on stone and marble.

Sensible eating

For the visitor to India, perhaps the most persistent worry will be whether or not the spices in the food will upset the stomach and, if one does not like curried food, what alternatives are there to eat.

If you really do not like curry (some people are prejudiced by the thought, not the deed), then there are many alternatives available either by asking the tour manager or the hotel reception. There is no need to eat spicy food, ask for 'boily-food' (as the cook will refer to unspiced food). Many Indians prefer to eat this themselves, so asking for it will cause no fuss in the kitchens. In Kashmir the spices are very bland but exciting and delicious enough to tempt the most conservative palate. For peace of mind try to remember the following three rules:

> *do not add ice to anything outside the hotel*
> *do not eat any ice-cream*
> *do not eat any fresh fruit which you yourself have not peeled*

If you follow these injunctions, then your stomach will almost certainly be fine. The water in the container in your bedroom will be quite alright to drink. Never buy drinks that are in the bottles with marbles in the top, the seal will be imperfect and the contents suspect.

For a short stay in Kashmir, which applies to anywhere in India, avoid ice-cream unless you are a guest at a private party or staying at a reputable hotel. Ice-cream is very tempting in a hot climate and Indians eat it by the ton. Only that of a reputable maker, or served at the hotel would be safe. Do not buy from a street vendor.

Bananas are, perhaps, the most ubiquitous fruit and are good for the stomach and come ready-wrapped, so to speak. Oranges are the same, they too can be peeled and will quench a thirst. Limes are plentiful all over India and can be squeezed into soda water or used to make water-tablet-purified water more palatable. All other fruit should be avoided: dates, sultanas, plums, melon slices; all apples should be washed and peeled and grapes thoroughly washed before eating.

Indian cooking skills have been handed down from mother to daughter, father to son, and from cook to cook, and each community or sect will have its own traditions. All over India a variety of cooking will be found that has evolved over the centuries, influenced by the traditions of Hindu, Muslim, Christian, Parsee, Sikh and European.

The cow is sacred to the Hindus, for whom it is anathema to think of it as food. For the Muslim the pig is despicable and similarly shunned as a food source, though for quite different reasons. Whilst not all Hindus are orthodox, most Muslims are. The Christians will eat any kind of meat, but abattoirs in India are the prerogative of one sect and are often primitive places, not controlled by the health authorities. Vegetarian food, therefore, is a natural alternative.

Vegetarian food in India is very different from the Western idea. It has no overtones of 'slimming' and 'good health', but is more a way of life. From a dietary point of view it can sometimes be so rich as to produce obesity. This state of 'largeness' is attractive to many Indians and there are many really large people who live entirely on vegetarian food.

Meat is tenderised and cooked in spices and in yoghurt or juices and is presented in an endless variety of ways. A clever cook can transform the toughest goat-meat into something delectable. Lamb or mutton on a menu will nearly always mean goat, except in Kashmir where there are plenty of sheep. Pork can be found but is eaten by very few people. Wild pig roam around many areas and will be eaten especially by the Sikhs.

It is not necessary for a curry to be spice-hot. In fact, mild curries are found more than the fiercely hot ones. Basically, southern cooking will be hotter with chillies than northern cooking, and there will also be more vegetarianism in the south. Tandoori cooking need not be hot and neither will much of the Kashmiri cooking. If, when ordering a meal, you are wary of the spice, of the hotness, ask the waiter to bring you a sample of the 'sauce' (they might call it 'gravy') and then you will know if you are going to enjoy it. If the food is too bland then ask for some chilli sauce and mix it into the food at the table.

Alcoholic drinks are available in Kashmir and the Indian-made whiskeys, gin and vodka are fine and go down very well with the sun! Imported spirits are very expensive. Indian brandy would be best left in the shop but the rum, probably made in Bhutan, is excellent. There are an increasing number of 'imitation' fortified wines but they are foolishly expensive and would only please the palate of the most confirmed toper. Indian beer is very good and is the safest and most quenching of alcoholic drinks. In Kashmir, buy a bottle of a cordial called Ruafsa. It is a pink, thick, cordial-syrup much enjoyed by Muslims and when added to water makes an exotic alternative to squashes.

For emergency situations, when stuck somewhere without liquid, then, apart from chewing a stone (not advisable), keep in the corner of a pocket or handbag a few cloves or cardamon pods or a little stick of cinnamon and you will have something to suck until you reach the bar!

Kashmiri food

The variety of food available in Jammu and Kashmir is as extensive as in any other State in India, or, for that matter, any other particular country.

What you eat depends on what you like or, very often, what you *think* you like, for food prejudice among tourists is something quite natural – a fear of the unknown or of eating something that will not agree with one – so that all too often it can spoil a visit to a country.

Fortunately Kashmir has a long-standing tradition of catering for 'The British' (in other words, for the European taste) in its varied types of cuisine. Being such a legendary place, Kashmir has attracted travellers from all over the world for years and has catered for these differing tastes.

One can eat Chinese-style in many places, including Indian restaurants, which tend to cater for both Chinese and Indian types of food. There are, too, the pizza bars and, if one must, the fish and chip cafes; also there are the general European-type restaurants where one can have brown Windsor soup and roast beef and spotted dick pudding. It would be a pity, though, to go so far and not experience real Kashmiri cooking, which is delicious, palatable, digestable and very varied.

A typical Kashmiri meal would consist of dishes made from mutton or chicken, served with rice and bread. Local specialities are things such as biryanis – lamb or chicken cooked together with rice and spices and sometimes topped with fruit and nuts and, on special occasions, finished off with a leaf of silver. Gustaba is another dish – a meatball curry eaten with lots of plain boiled rice. Muttar panir is cubes of cheese cooked with peas in a thick rich gravy. Gabargah usually has lamb cut up and cooked slowly over a slow heat and has such spices as cloves and cardamon and cinnamon mixed into the gravy. Skewered lamb meat or chicken meat, called kebab, is most popular and eaten a lot when cooking over a camp fire whilst off trekking.

A speciality around Kashmir is trout, either caught fresh by sportsmen who have a fishing licence, or produced commercially for the many restaurants. It can be served curried – an unusual dish and more delicious than one might think – or can be eaten Western-style, grilled or fried. There are plenty of 'tandoori' eating places, but enquire first if they really have a tandoor, a clay oven kept especially for tandoori cooking; then you will be sure to be getting the correctly cooked food. There are so many imitations of 'tandoori' cooking, mainly because of its increased popularity in the West so that, in the West, shortcuts are the order of the day and there are few real Indian clay tandoors (clay ovens) in Europe.

One can eat vegetarian food at many places and your cook boat attached to the houseboat will prepare vegetarian dishes if you desire. These houseboat cooks will be very much at home cooking Western food, often referred to as 'boily-food', as they and their families have been cooking these dishes for Europeans for decades.

Duck is on most menus wherever you eat and will certainly be a part of food suggested by your houseboat-boy. Rarer, but very appetising, is casseroled pigeons, cooked either in a wine sauce or in the Indian way, or Kashmiri way to be exact, in a spicy sauce and served with vegetables rather than rice.

Kashmiri drinks are sometimes too perfumed for the Western taste. One thinks of the cordial Ruafsa, bought as bottled syrup and diluted with water or soda water. It is a lovely pink colour and tastes of roses! More refreshing is lime water, or mosambi juice. A mosambi is like a large orange and tastes rather thin but is a good and safe drink and, with a pinch of salt added, revives one well after a scorching time in the sun. A sherbert is made out of fried rose petals, sugar and rosewater, called Sharbat gulab; another is made from sandalwood powder, sugar and rosewater, called Sharbat sandal; both are exotic and have to be ordered.

Kashmiri tea is ubiquitous throughout the Valley. There are two kinds and each is usually drunk after meals. One is salty and rather dark brown and not very attractive. One needs to be specific, therefore, to have the one most suitable to the Western palate. This is Kashmiri sweet tea and is made by infusing green tea leaves, cardamon pods, a small piece of cinnamon and, variably, almonds, or cloves according to the whim of the servant. Green tea is the tea leaf after it has been plucked and before it has been subjected to the drying process that turns it black. It has a sweetly bitter flavour which is more gentle than cured tea and the spices impart a delicate refreshing flavour. It is also a digestive, hence it is drunk after meals.

Needless to say in so fertile an area, fruit is in plentiful supply and great variety. Apples, pears, pomegranates, strawberries, mulberries, apricots

Apple picking on the road to Srinagar

and peaches are some that are grown locally, and many others are imported into Kashmir, such as oranges and lemons, which grow further south.

Lastly, there is Kashmiri honey, more often than not said to be lotus honey (but who can control the collecting instincts of the bee?!). All the honey is thick, very sweet and has an individual aroma. Some cafés sell baked apples whose core is filled with honey and pine nuts.

Ice

Throughout India there are ice factories which turn out blocks of ice in great quantities. The water from which the ice is made may be quite pure and filtered by the local water authority. It is what happens to the ice on the way from the factory to the consumer that makes it dangerous, and adding it to drinks of any kind can soon produce the unwelcome signs of tummy trouble.

The blocks of ice are transported on hand-carts or by rickshaw or even by bullock cart and the ice is broken up on the street or filthy pavement. Often it is wrapped in sacking so that a passer-by would not realise that the contents are ice. With the sacking ripped open the blocks will be dragged through all sorts of imaginable dirt until it reaches the restaurant or stall or small hotel and, after some time, is added to a drink. This drink spells danger!

Not all ice comes from the ice factory. Much is made under hygienic conditions by hotels, especially those in the upper price bracket who cater for the foreign visitor. Tours, though, often mingle hotels in order to cut costs and whereas 'night one' may be spent in luxury, 'night two' might be in a slightly down-grade hotel, and in these lesser hotels the ice could be contaminated and therefore it is better to steer clear of consuming it.

A change from drinking water is to order a 'nimboo pani', literally lime-water. It will be made from fresh limes, sugar and a pinch of salt and goes well with curry and spicy meals – but remember, no ice.

6 Festivals and fairs

Festivals

A festival in India will, more often than not, be connected in some way with a faith. India has seen the birth of three of the important religions of the world – Hinduism, Buddhism and Jainism – and many others have become established in the country and have flourished in India's unique climate of religious toleration. Two such are Christianity and Islam.

India has the second largest Muslim population in the world, a population from which have emerged many great men, such as Akbar, the Moghul Emperor, for instance, who sponsored Persian translations of the great Hindu epics, the *Ramayana* and the *Mahabharata*.

Christianity spread to India earlier than most everywhere else outside the Middle East. Its influence, plus that of the predominant Muslim community, and the Hindus, though disparate, form the main cultures of the Valley and of Srinagar.

Throughout India all religions enjoy full equality and the followers of each faith celebrate their feasts in a bewildering number of annual festivals. Many of the Hindu holidays are linked with harvest and seemingly every change of season is celebrated in song and dance. Other holidays honour mythological deities or are entirely religious, involving fasting and special prayers.

It is not likely, therefore, that a visitor to India, and Kashmir in particular, will miss being able to join in or witness some festival; he need only be in the right place at the right time!

There follows a list of festivals arranged from January to December and the places where it is most likely that they can be enjoyed; only approximate dates are given as so many depend on the moon. The list will be useful to those travellers who wish to extend their experience beyond the State of Jammu and Kashmir.

January

Pongal, or Sankranti   Celebrated throughout Tamil Nadu, Andhra Pradesh and Karnataka in the south but almost all over India. In the south, though, it is a very big occasion when the sun is worshipped, the houses cleaned, special pongal rice is cooked and the cows and bullocks are part of the festivities. On the third day of pongal, in some southern towns, there are bull-fights in which young men try to wrest bundles of currency notes from the horns of ferocious bulls. The bulls are not killed for they will, eventually, return to their life of toil behind the plough. This bull-fighting is called Jallikattu, especially to be seen around Madurai and Trichinopoly, now called Tiruchiripalli.

Republic Day   This national festival of India is observed throughout the country to mark the inauguration of the Republic of India on 26 January 1950. In Delhi the celebrations include a magnificent parade of the armed forces and of civilians from all States. The parade ends with a fly-past of zooming planes and 'dancing' helicopters. The President of India takes the salute, whilst in the State, where there are also separate parades, the Governor of the State takes the salute. If you are in New Delhi at this time try and reserve a seat as it is one procession in which you will see bejewelled elephants and the once famous Camel Corps.

Sivratri   Celebrated by Hindus all over India, Sivratri is a festival devoted to the worship of Lord Siva. Devotees spend the night singing songs in his praise. Special celebrations are held at important temples such as those at Chidambaram, Varanasi (Benares), Kalahasti and Kharjuraho.

Bakr-Id or Id-ul-Zuha   A festival to commemorate the Prophet Ibrahim offering his son for sacrifice. Rams and goats are sacrificed and new clothes are worn and there is feasting and rejoicing.

February

Muharam   This commemorates the martyrdom of Iman Hussain, the grandson of the Prophet Mohammed. Tazias, which are symbolic of the martyr's tomb at Karbala, are carried in mourning processions. The most famous Muharram procession is to be seen at Lucknow (see earlier on Islamic religion, p. 22).

March

Holi   The most boisterous of India's festivals, it is observed all over northern India. Men, women and children throw coloured water and powder over one another. Sweetmeats are exchanged between friends. If you don't mind being squirted with water and colour then brave the

Parade, Srinagar

streets; and brave is the appropriate word. Any European would be a special target and enthusiasm often overcomes commonsense.

The crowds are dense and items quite different from coloured water are often thrown by the vulgar. European women should not go out into the streets. Visitors may celebrate Holi in a delightful way within the confines of their hotel or, if staying with a family, as advised by them.

In Rajasthan, at Jaipur, the Holi Elephant Festival is now held. A procession makes its way through the streets to the Changan Stadium, made up of elephants caparisoned and decked with jewels and painted

A Hindu temple ceremonial car

howdahs. To see this event is to witness a little of India's fabulous and indulgent past. Beside the procession there are polo matches, races, dancing and song competitions. It is a very gay time, strikingly colourful, radiant and dazzling and, if the beautiful city of Jaipur could be enhanced, then during Holi it is. Jammu and Kashmir, Srinagar in particular, have their own celebrations but these are mostly family affairs. It is quite possible to combine a visit first to Rajasthan and then go up to Srinagar.

May
Buddha Purnima   Celebrating the birth, enlightenment, death and salvation of the Lord Buddha. This festival is especially relevant in the State of Bihar.

June/July
Car Festival   This is the time when temple cars, huge wooden structures on wheels which carry the God, make their processions. The most famous and spectacular is at Puri, in Orissa, when over a million people cram the route to see Lord Jaganath being pulled in the enormous temple chariot by teams of volunteer men. Once, devotees would throw themselves under the wheels of the chariots and kill themselves, thus attaining Nirvanah.

This suicide is now banned. If going to Kashmir from Calcutta then this is an ideal time as the Valleys will be warm and the Car Festival can be witnessed *en route*.

August

Independence Day – 15 August   This is the anniversary of India's independence from British Rule in 1947. There are no special celebrations but the Prime Minister makes a speech from the ramparts of the Red Fort at New Delhi. The event is televised to the nation.

Onam   The greatest festival in the State of Kerala, Onam is primarily a harvest festival. It is observed in every home and in open public places. There will be some evidence of this festival in Kashmir at the homes of south Indians in particular.

Janmasthami   The birth of Lord Krishna, believed to be the reincarnation of Vishnu and author of the *Bhagavadgita*. This festival is celebrated all over India but especially at Mathura and Brindavan (Mysore), where Lord Krishna spent his childhood. In Bombay, New Delhi and at Agra special performances are enacted, often by children, of scenes from Lord Krishna's early life.

October

Gandhi Jayanti   The anniversary of the birth of Mahatma Gandhi, celebrated throughout the land. At the Rajghat, New Delhi, where Gandhi's body was cremated, there is a special ceremony with prayers.

Dussera, or Durga Puja   This is a ten-day festival based on the epic *Ramayana*, signifying the triumph of good over evil. It is, perhaps, the most popular festival in India. Every region observes the festival in some way. In northern India it is known as Ram Lila and there are plays and presentations of dance and music recalling the doings of the legendary hero of the Ramayana, Rama. On the tenth day processions collect at public grounds, there to burn the often enormous effigies of Ravana, which will be stuffed with fireworks that will explode before thousands of spectators. It is in West Bengal that this festival is known as Durga Puja, since the Goddess Durga aided Rama in his defeat of Ravana, and Calcutta is the principal place to witness this extraordinary event; the food, too, will be special and marvellous.

Dussera festival – effigies of Ravana, Kumbkarna and Mekhnath ready for destruction

Holi festival – throwing the colours

November

Diwali This is an occasion for great rejoicing and excitement and is, perhaps, the happiest of Indian festivals, when innumerable lamps are lit in niches and windows and on pavements and in trees and floated on lakes and down streams and rivers. The lights are symbolic of lamps lit to show Rama his way home from his many adventures. This festival is also dedicated to the Goddess Lakshmi, particularly in Bombay and in the State of Gujarat. Here it will be very noisy for at least ten days and nights. The people let off fireworks and loud bangers. Businessmen vie with each other to set off the loudest and most continuous series of bangs. It is a propitious way of saluting the Goddess Lakshmi, who happens to be the Goddess of wealth! Travellers arriving in Bombay would be well advised to carry ear plugs with them.

In Bengal they worship the Goddess Kali, she who symbolises strength. Spectacular images of Kali are made and worshipped and then immersed in a river or in some convenient water.

Coming right on top of the Dussera festivities this is an interesting time to be in India and, perhaps, something to consider seeing after having been up to Srinagar for an autumn visit.

Id-ul-Fitr, Ramadan   This Muslim festival marks the end of Ramadan, the Muslim month of fasting and is an occasion for feasting and rejoicing. The mosques are full and so are homes, being visited by friends and relatives exchanging good wishes and greetings. The festival is a movable one, varying in date from year to year. All over Jammu and Kashmir there will be celebrations, seldom seen by visitors, who by November will have left the Vale and its charms.

December

Feast of St Xavier   Celebrated on December 3rd, this is one of the most important festivals in Goa. It marks the mission of St Xavier in India. Special masses are said in the churches and there are religious processions. Christians of Kashmir will celebrate this in their churches.

Christmas time   Christmas is observed in much splendour throughout the churches in India with carol singing and, especially in Goa and Daman and in the southern States, by colourful processions. Pageants are staged telling the story of Christmas, but, unlike in the West and in Kashmir, in the south the sun will be shining. In Bombay a Pontifical High Mass is held in the open air at the Cooperage Gardens. In New Delhi services are held at the Sacred Heart Church and at St Paul's Cathedral. Christmas Day is a declared holiday all over India.

Fairs

As distinct from festivals, fairs have very much a business air, not being governed by any religious event. They are a periodical gathering for the sale of goods, often with entertainment, exhibitions and quite a lot of chicanery.

The most colourful of fairs is at Pushkar, 11 km (7 miles) from Ajmer in Rajasthan. The fair is noted for the sale of camels. Races are held in which riders on gaily decorated camels show off the speed and manoeuvrability of their mounts. On the final day of the Pushkar Fair, prizes are awarded and a kind of musical chairs is played by the camel riders. Many tours take in this event. November is the time and it can be cold, especially at night. If visiting Kashmir and combining this event then the appropriate clothing will serve both centres – warm woollens and a warm top coat or raincoat.

Another fair which is similar to the Pushkar Fair is held at Sonepur, a small township situated on the banks of the Ganges near Patna in the State of Bihar. This is intended for the sale of cattle not camels. It is a very basic affair but makes an interesting stop *en route* to Kashmir from, say, Calcutta.

Another fair is determined by a solar eclipse and is celebrated in

A trade fair

northern centres like Allahabad, Hardwar, Varanasi (Benares) and especially at Kurukshetra, in Haryana State. A solar eclipse is an occasion when pious Hindus bathe in rivers and pay homage to their ancestors. Thousands of pilgrims congregate at rivers all over India, especially along the length of the Ganges. It is amazing that so many people will immerse themselves joyously in waters that are often chill and uninviting.

7 Houseboats

Houseboats became a part of the Kashmir scene because the ruler of Kashmir forbade the British to own land in Kashmir. The resourceful British, though, perhaps remembering experiences on the Thames at Henley, thought of houseboats, which would not infringe the rule, and so founded one of the great traditions without which, it is arguable, the economy of the Valley of Kashmir would greatly suffer.

Some houseboats are built with rooms running into each other, separated in the middle by a main entrance and galley; others have rooms leading off a corridor which runs the entire length, ending in a pantry. All, though, will differ in some way or another and all are delightful and enchanting and extremely comfortable.

The large boats can be as much as 55 m (180 ft) long and 3.6–4.3 m (12–14 ft) wide. Houseboats in the main have square ends, the rear being used for a water boiler which is stoked with logs and wood chippings and provides running hot water to the bathrooms, morning and evening. The front end is a verandah, often with landing steps leading up from the water. These verandahs are spacious and are made of intricately carved woodwork; from them one can sit and watch boatmen, traders – and kingfishers.

The interior, depending on the category, will be either opulent or comfortable. Houseboat categories are Delux, A, B, C and D, and some will sport any number of stars as a rating. These should be disregarded, as star rating is not part of the officially licensed categories – it just looks good and is fun.

The difference in houseboats is that the Delux will be lit by chandeliers, have plush furniture and large bedrooms and tiled Western-style bathrooms; they are really luxurious. These trimmings are less opulent as one goes from A through to D class. These latter will be comfortable in a more humble way, lit probably by pink glass shields over wall lights, have 1930s-style large arm chairs, and will be smaller in girth and length, yet will have all the facilities such as service and a pantry and running hot and cold water.

Houseboats and water-skiing on Lake Dal

Most boats will be carpeted by Persian rugs, many of them quite old and all beautiful. The furniture will most probably be of teak, the walls and ceilings of pine. In the upper-class boats walnut will be used for small tables and other items, and divisions between sitting-room and, say, bedroom will be made of screens of carved wood panels.

Many houseboats have open fires and these can be lit, at a small extra charge, on chilly nights. Other boats have a kind of free-standing stove which burns wood and smells wonderful, and quickly warms the living area. On these cool nights a shawl is most welcome so, rather than wait until leaving to buy one, buy one as soon as you arrive and use it where it was meant to be used.

Delux boats will have three or four bedrooms, each with its own bathroom, and one has to marvel at there being so much hot water supplied by what seems to be an inadequate boiler. Category B and C class boats are a joy. Less important and opulent, yet with every bit as good a position around the lake as many of the more expensive boats, they are smaller, cozy, and can be rented only for oneself, that is to say exclusively for one's own use.

Houseboats have a roof space railed off and overhung by an awning. This is the sun-bathing terrace, a fine place for an evening drink or meal, but somewhere to avoid in the summertime as the heat can be overpowering even under the awning. The high altitude atmosphere, as in Switzerland, allows all the power of the sun to beam down, and one can get very burnt very quickly.

Around the boat there will be a cat-walk and one can often hear the pad of bare feet as the house-boy goes around on some errand. All the houseboats have wire mesh at the windows because of mosquitoes, which are especially bothersome at night. If your boy sprays the rooms whilst you are out with a repellent and you keep the windows closed you will not experience discomfort. July and August are fairly bad times; if you go in late April, May and the first half of June then you will not be troubled.

The houseboats are moored to either island or river bank by chains, wires or ropes and roll only in a bad storm. From this mooring electricity power supply cables are led, usually via the rear of the boat, and there will be a rising water tap for general outside use. All boats are provided with water that is treated and filtered by the Kashmiri Government Water Board so that it is drinkable.

Most boats have a supply of magazines and books and all will have a writing desk complete with writing paper and envelopes, called, throughout India, 'covers'. The furniture will be English-style and there will be an array of table silver, cruets, napkin rings, sugar bowls, etc, table cloths and a dining-room that is the pride of the houseboat-boy. He is the main-stay of any time on a houseboat. He will see to laundry, clean the boat, make the beds and pamper you by putting hot water bottles in your bed before you retire, a comfort that will be welcome if there in April and October.

Behind the houseboat will be moored the cook-boat and it is from here that all meals will be provided. Your boy will ask you at breakfast for the menu for the day, so it is as well to be prepared. European food is readily available, but the Kashmiri food is so delicious that it should form a part of your experience; also, they know how to cook their way better than your way.

It used to be quite a regular thing to see a houseboat being towed from its moorings to another lake position and, though this can still be done, the need is less as many new boats have been built around the lake and other

Houseboat with cookboat behind

lakes, like Nagin Lake, so that it is better to hire a boat where you want it rather than go to the expense of having yours towed.

During the summer season the lakes can get crowded. If you wish a quiet time, go early when it will be peaceful and calm.

You should tip your houseboat-boy and shikara-boy and, if the food has been excellent, the cook.

Shikara punts, houseboats, and hotel in left background

8 Temples, shrines and gardens

The pilgrim trail

Throughout centuries Kashmir has attracted saints, gurus and holy men, many of whom are today venerated at shrines scattered all over the area. The two main faiths of Islam and Hinduism have found great expression in Kashmir and all through the year pilgrims pay homage, especially at the main shrines in the valley. Here are details of some of these.

Hazratbal Dargah

The perfect proportions of this white marble shrine, which stands on the western bank of Lake Dal, are reflected beautifully in the lake water. The Dargah has a special sanctity because of the sacred hair of the Prophet Mohammed, which is enshrined in the inner sanctum. This holy relic is displayed on several occasions each year.

Shankaracharya Temple

This temple dominates the skyline of Srinagar and the lakes. It is built on top of the Takht-i-Sulaiman hill and is believed to be one of the oldest Hindu shrines in the Valley that is dedicated to Lord Siva. The temple is believed to have been constructed around 200 BC. Having climbed up the hill to the temple one is rewarded with spectacular views of Srinagar and its surroundings. The top is approachable, too, by a roadway leading to the television transmitter tower, an unfortunate addition to what was a perfect backdrop.

Amanath

Sited 45 km (28 miles) from Pahalgam, and 141 km (88 miles) from Srinagar, and situated at a height of 3800 m (12,460 ft) in the upper reaches of the Himalayas, the origins of this temple are lost in antiquity. There is historical evidence that a pilgrimage was made there as far back as 1000 BC. Each year, on the night of the full moon of July–August, pilgrims walk this long trek from Pahalgam and gather at the sacred cave in thousands. At that height the weather is freezing. According to belief,

Lord Siva revealed here the mystery of the Maya and salvation to Parvati, on a full-moon night in summertime.

Kir Bhawani

43 km (27 miles) from Srinagar a sacred spring rises at the village of Tula Mula. Here is a marble temple venerated by Hindus. On the eighth day of the full moon in the month of May, fasting devotees gather to seek the blessings of the goddess Ragnaya Devi. At a certain time it is said that the waters change colour.

Vaishno Devi

High above the plains of Jammu, approachable by a road and then a 14 km (9 mile) trek, is the cave shrine of the goddess Vaishno Devi. The cave is 30 m (98 ft) long and very narrow, with ice-cold waters flowing through it. The far end of the cave has three rock formations covered with gold canopies. These represent the three divine aspects of the goddess.

Charari Sharief

The Ziarat of Sheikh Nur-ud-din, popularly called Kashmir's patron saint, is situated 28 km (17 miles) south of Srinagar. The saint, who is venerated by both Muslims and Hindus, was the founder of a Muslim order of rishis, holy men, whose aim was to serve the community and spread the message of peace. The shrine has a tiered roof resting on wooden pillars.

Shahdra Sharief

32 km (20 miles) from Rajouri in Jammu is this Muslim shrine known as Shahdra Sharief, which has grown around the tomb of the Muslim saint, Pir Ghulam Shah.

The Moghul gardens

Well over 300 years ago, around 1619, the Emperor Jehangir laid out the Shalimar Garden for the personal delight of his wife, Nur Jahan. Throughout the following centuries this garden has become synonymous with feelings both romantic and oriental.

High among the Himalayan mountains, far away from even the East, let alone the West, travellers once needed to undertake a journey of considerable fortitude and perseverance to reach its setting in the Vale of Kashmir. With the advent of such communications as railways and metalled roads this whole area became comparatively easy of access and its fame spread accordingly, eventually inspiring one of the Western world's most well-known parlour songs. The 'Kashmiri Song' is one of a set of four poems entitled 'The Garden of Kama' by Laurence Hope and was set to music by Amy Woodforde-Finden. The first line runs: 'Pale hands I loved beside the Shalimar . . .'.

Once it took weeks of journeying to reach Kashmir whereas now one can be there, walking among the avenues of the Shalimar Garden, within hours, from almost anywhere in the world. Shalimar means 'the abode of love', popularly translated from the Sanskrit.

As with all Moghul gardens the ground plan is that of a grid with criss-crossing and terracing, through the centre of which runs a water course. Water and shade are the two essentials that give these gardens their particular character. At the Shalimar Garden the water is harnessed from a natural spring, or 'nullah', a small stream. This water is fed into the system of water courses and activates fountains and rills and cascades over stones carved to resemble fish-scales. The water flows through pools and under stepping stones with a magical tinkling sound, cooling the air and adding calm beneath the tall chenar trees. All around are colourful flower-beds full of flowers associated with the English summer borders.

The Shalimar Garden is set back from the shore of Lake Dal and is approached by a small canal. To arrive there by shikara boat has the same charm as does arriving by gondola somewhere along the canals of Venice. The Royal Garden of Shalimar, as it is properly called, has a large central pavilion with exquisitely carved pillars of black marble. It is set within a tank of water in which play numbers of fountains; it is called the Diwan-i-Am, the audience hall, where the Emperor Jehangir and his successors used to sit so that his people could see him. The garden is 540 m (600 yd) long and has three pavilions, the one nearest the mountains and farthest from the lake being the Diwan-i-Khas, the hall of private audience, with, behind it, several rooms for domestic use. The Ladies Garden is the most beguiling of all, with its black marble pavilion, another one, from which channels of water run at right angles through beds of flowers.

Another Moghul Garden, quite near the Shalimar Garden, is the Nishat Bagh, Garden of Delight. One can arrive here either directly from the houseboat by shikara to the landing stage, or by road, walking or on local transport. One of the most beautiful things here is the arrangement of lilac hedging which, when in bloom in the springtime, smells heavenly. A lattice-windowed wooden pavilion stands in the centre of one terrace inside which used to play a geometric display of fountains and water jets. The garden is surrounded by a high wall and has a series of terraces which run beneath shady trees and beds of pyrethrum, French marigolds, stocks, roses and all manner of summer flowers.

Birds abound in all the gardens and at any one time will be seen a bulbul or a babbler or a hoopoe, a white barred brown bird with a crest and a curved beak for probing the ground for insects. The red vented bulbul also

Shalimar Garden

has a crest and flits among the lower branches of trees and shrubs. Watch out particularly for the scarlet minivets. They fly high up through the trees catching insects, are quite small and radiantly coloured.

From these gardens, the Shalimar and the Nishat, there are lovely views of Lake Dal and the surrounding mountains. Over to the right in the distance, reflected in the still waters, rises the mighty Nanga Parbat.

Another garden is called the Chashma Shahi Bagh which lies to the north of Shankaracharya Hill, the local hill which dominates the valley. Here is probably the most charming of the Moghul gardens.

Fine views are to be had from here of the lake and mountains, the

houseboats and floating gardens and of all life on the water, over as far as the Char Chenar. This small island in the middle of Lake Dal comprises four chenar trees, with a small pavilion in the middle which was a summer-house for the Emperors and their ladies. Once this summer-house had a silver roof and the island was called 'Silver Island'.

The Chashma Shahi Garden was laid out in 1632 by the Emperor Shah Jehan. Its name means 'The Royal Spring'. The original garden has now been extended to accommodate visitors as it is the smallest of the Moghul gardens. It consists of a summer-house and pavilion and terraces of trees and flowers, and the spring. The spring water which feeds the garden freezes the hand if held under at its source, and the water is reputed to have medicinal properties. There are lawns and high walls and beds of flowers and, according to Moghul custom, there is a central waterway with fountains and channels. The pavilion is a useful place in more ways than one for even on summer days there can be a sudden sharp downfall of rain and it affords welcome shelter.

Immediately above the Chashma Shahi Garden is the Pari Mahal, an old Muslim college. Now ruined, its arched terraces and arcades present marvellous and very photogenic views of the lake. From here there is a direct road or pathway to the lakeside.

At the Chashma Shahi Gardens one can stay at tourist cabins, and there is a restaurant; it is, too, the only garden for which there is an entry charge.

Whatever the beauty of these gardens, their ingenuity, their magic or the legends related about them, they are overshadowed by the incredible grandeur and magnificence of their setting in the Vale of Kashmir.

Moghul garden with background of Himalayan hills

9 Kashmiri carpets, rugs and souvenirs

Carpets and rugs

There is a misunderstanding in the West that, in order to weave a carpet or rug, 'slave labour' is employed, most of which consists of young boys. The misunderstanding comes with the word 'slave'; only in certain cases where bondage is prevalent – amongst, for instance, backward farming communities and where tribals exist – can the term 'slave' be used. The custom of bondage does not exist in Kashmir.

For any member of a family to be in work is better than for none to be in work and the earning, no matter how small, adds to the family's income without which many would go hungry. This applies to workers in any of the cottage industries, from match-making in the south of India to silk-weaving along the Ganges. Income, whatever the pittance, is of the greatest importance. To change the customs and habits of centuries in forty years of independence is not possible, and may not be desirable, especially in a country whose population is doubling at an alarming rate.

One has to understand the worker, be it girl, boy or man, to understand the weavers and the sales merchants and also know about deep-seated family traditions which are much older and more secure in the long run than are the affluent well-paid Western ways. In this way one will, perhaps, accept the image of 'little boys' sitting in 'cramped conditions' working for 'a few rupees daily' as reported by journalists. In only a few cases are such stories factual. The majority of hand carpet weavers are correctly paid, proud of their job, philosophical about the profits made after manufacture and glad of the employment in the factory.

Explanation might be best made here of the term 'factory'. This word is applied to any small business which produces something and is very often only a small building of concrete or wood or brick, housing either workers or varying amounts of machinery. In almost all cases where people work producing goods or giving a service the name for their place of work will be 'factory'. The term is used in the same way as is 'hotel', which can mean anything from a tea stall to the Sheraton Hotel.

Although there are quite large factories producing carpets in Kashmir there are far more individual family weavers. These families have been weaving carpets in wool, wool and silk or in pure silk for centuries, passing on traditions from father to son. They work mostly during the long winter months when the Valley is cut off and is freezing in sub-zero temperatures.

Until the Industrial Revolution and the great exhibitions in London and Paris the carpet weaving industry in Kashmir ebbed and flowed with the varying demands from rulers and merchants. Western taste sought carpets from Persia and Afghanistan – from places such as Tabriz, Kashan and the like. The British gave sporadic orders for rugs and carpets for houseboats and bungalows, but it was not until after the Prince of Wales' visit in 1875, after a special carpet had been woven for use during his stay at Jammu, that there was an awakening of interest in the Kashmir craftsmanship. Sensing quick profits, Europeans in Kashmir started a factory, which really was worthy of the name, and is reputed to have employed 'thousands' of weavers. This factory supplied rugs, runners and carpets to the great families of Europe and won coveted awards by showing at exhibitions. This commerce thankfully gave the Kashmiri carpets a lasting place in the showrooms all over the world, so that they competed well with those made in Persia, Turkey and Afghanistan, at the same time repeating the old traditional patterns of these places.

With two world wars interrupting trading, the fortunes of the Kashmiri weavers suffered. Few carpets or rugs came out of India until, encouraged by the State Government and the Central Government, weaving increased steadily, as did tourism, so that now the carpet weaving industry is, perhaps, Kashmir's main export commodity.

The ancient ways are still used to produce these attractive and time-enduring carpets. On a loom a weaver will weave a pattern according to the call of his assistant who will be reading from a written pattern. Coloured balls of wool hang down above the weaver or knotter and as the colours are called so will he pull the wool, thread and knot it and cut it. Cotton thread is knotted after each row has been finished to secure the wool. After about six weeks work, depending on size, the pile of the rug will be cut with shears to an even length. The carpet or rug is then immersed in water, most often in a nearby river or stream, or in the lake, and it is washed so that all dye excess is removed and the knots are tightened. After drying and combing, the lustrous colours will glow and the depth of the pile be regular.

When buying a rug or carpet, ask for the number of knots per square metre. A good one will have 400,000 knots in a square metre. After buying you will be given a certificate of authenticity on which the number of knots is shown. The less the number of knots, the less important the carpet, and the cheaper it will be. One is expected to bargain and a reasonable price can usually be arrived at by comparing three different dealers and their 'last' prices.

The variety is bewildering and choosing will be difficult. Buy a silk carpet for hanging on the wall and a wool, or wool and silk, for the floor. Try and read about rugs and carpets before going to Kashmir and remember designs and names like Shiraz, Kashan, Ispahan, Na'in and Bokhara; it may help in selecting.

Providing the luggage allowance is not exceeded, small wool-pile rugs and such items as 'numda' rugs can be carried home by hand. Should this not be feasible then rugs and carpets can be despatched via air freight from Kashmir to any destination in the world.

Craft souvenirs

Papier-mâché

The papier-mâché work of Kashmir is appreciated by most visitors as a souvenir of their holiday. Examples that are being made today are unrivalled for their delicacy and intricate patterns and their glowing colours. There will be few who will leave Kashmir without taking with them some item of papier-mâché work.

Nowadays it is difficult, if not impossible, to buy a real Kashmir papier-mâché article because modern demand has brought with it short cuts in production. To understand the difference between a genuine piece of papier-mâché work and one which, though charming, is spurious, it is needful to know something of the history and craftsmanship of papier-mâché making, originally known in Kashmir as Kari-i-Qualmdani (a qualmdan being a sort of pencil or pen box, which were the first articles made in papier-mâché).

Papier-mâché is repulped paper which, when mixed with an appropriate glue, can be moulded, dried and, when quite hard, decorated and lacquered. The term 'papier-mâché' is French and means, literally, mashed paper, and may first have been used by French emigré workers in England.

The customary way of making papier-mâché is by soaking waste paper in water for upwards of twenty days. Special paper is eagerly sought and many craftsmen have arrangements to procure the waste from such places as paper mills or stationers and printers. The soaked paper is squeezed and is then put into a container, customarily of stone, and is pounded to a fine paste into which is mixed rice flour or some other glue agent. This pulp is left to mature whilst suitable wooden moulds are being carved.

Around the mould are first placed strips of soaked paper forming a skin, then layers of paste followed by layers of fine muslin, for strength. The covered mould is left to dry in the sun, after which it is sawn in half and the papier-mâché skin removed and stuck together again. It looks grey and dirty until its surface is prepared for painting by first being rubbed smooth with a piece of burnt brick, called a karot, and then being coated with a glue mixed with lime. The surface is again smoothed with the karot, after which fine tissue-paper strips are applied which are afterwards coated with a white lead powder mixed with paste. The design or scene is then drawn free-hand in pencil onto a sheet of tissue-paper until each detail is correct, after which it is transfered to the article. It is the quality of this drawing, its excellence in style, and proportion, that will dictate the value of the finished article.

The ground colour is then applied as a free wash of colour, after which the box or vase will be decorated with a scene of Moghul court life, or of flowers or birds, and this decoration, like the whole process of the making of articles, will be undertaken by several members of one family. After the decoration a varnish is applied using either copal or amber powdered in linseed oil. For the cheaper pieces this is the final stage. For the more expensive ones this surface is rubbed time and again with wet grasses to erase any slight mounds or blemishes. It is at this stage that gold ornamentation is added and the completed article rubbed with a jade stone to brighten the colours and gold so that they will shine beneath a final coating of amber varnish.

The short-cut method of papier-mâché production is by making the wooden moulds and not removing them and re-gluing the actual papier-mâché. The wood is left inside and makes the whole thing heavy – one of the ways of telling a good piece being to test its weight with its size.

The finest examples of papier-mâché work combine a perfection of form and symmetry with a glass-smooth surface under which is an exquisitely coloured example of the painter's craft.

Beware of 'distressed' articles, those claimed to be 'very old Persian box' or 'centuries old'. Some dealers are adept at making an article look older than it is – metal, stonework, beads, papier-mâché, it doesn't matter; what matters about papier-mâché is its weight in relation to its whole, and its colours. A genuine old piece will have subdued shades mixed from powdered precious stones and will display conservative colours of dark red, pale blue and grey, and pale apple green. One would have to go to a specialist and trusted dealer to seek out such a piece. It is a case of *caveat emptor* and remember that items that are certified to be over 100 years old, anywhere in India, need a certificate and licence to export them – but the efforts will be very rewarding.

Part of a souvenir shop – the metal department

Shawls and shawl making

There are only two kinds of shawl – the 'pashmina' and all the rest. By the side of a genuine pashmina shawl all others pale, notwithstanding how beautifully they are woven or embroidered. The pashmina shawl is made from the rare underbelly wool of the pashmina goat.

The history of shawl making goes back to beyond biblical times. Travellers in the era of Solomon returned from the East with delicate beautiful shawls which had been made in Kashmir. It is said that Nero gave to a youth who had shown great daring and bravery in the ring at the Colosseum, 'a shawl from Cashmire of many colours and unsurpassable beauty'.

The word 'shawl' came into usage much later and seems to have been created by a merchant called Naqz-Beg. He was in service as a cook and gave a piece of Kashmiri pashmina wool, one and a half yards square, as a present for his master, calling it a 'shawl', the Persian word for blanket. From Istanbul to Afghanistan this word is used as 'shawlki', meaning an over-blanket.

There is a story that, via Egypt and the Napoleonic Wars, one rust-coloured shawl came into the possession of the Emperor Napoleon who passed it on to Josephine, and from that moment in history the shawl became a part of haute couture.

In modern times the first great period of pashmina shawl weaving was between 1865 and 1872, when craftsmanship, texture and material became of the finest that was possible. Those shawls made then are now the antique pashmina shawls for which high prices are paid; very few, though, come onto the market as they are family heirlooms and tend to be handed down through the years, especially among the Muslim families of Kashmir.

In the latter half of the nineteenth century a Scotsman named Kelso started to manufacture shawls called Paisley, after the town in Scotland that was famous for both factory and hand-weaving, and his mill-made copies of the original Kashmiri shawls quickly became commonplace. They became available to the masses at a quite different price from that charged for the 'real thing'. Those who had real pashmina shawls spread them over bed or piano, rather than risk wearing them too much, and they bought Kelso's copies for everyday wearing. This industry seemed not to affect the Kashmiri weavers as it was at this time that tourism began to flourish and so kept alive the local weaving industry.

The feeling of a pashmina shawl should be soft, warm, light and airy and the whole be capable of passing through a wedding-ring. The price you will have to pay for such a shawl will probably make you squirm; it will be in the thousands of rupees, and there is no substitute for the real thing. Before embarking on such an expensive purchase perhaps one should think as to how the shawl will eventually be used; they are a regular item of clothing in the cooler places in India but seldom seen these days as such in the West.

What makes the pashmina shawls so soft is the fine under-belly wool of the pashmina goats which inhabit the mountains leading from the upper valleys above Eastern Kashmir into the Tibetan heights. The higher up the goats live, the better the wool, as it will be naturally thicker, so producing extra warmth for the goat.

When the wool has been collected it is first carefully sorted and graded, then washed in a solution of rice-water, a process which keeps the wool's texture soft and leaves behind its natural oils. It is then spun and afterwards dyed and woven. Sometimes small pieces are woven which are later sewn together by hand; this method is called a 'kani' shawl. Any larger ones, over which will often be stitched intricate needlework patterns of geometric or flower designs, are called 'amlikar' shawls. When completed the shawls are washed in the water of either lake or river.

There are many other types of shawl for sale around the bazaars of Srinagar; made of ordinary wool, wool and silk, synthetic fibres or some of pure silk, none, though, will match the pashmina and yet all are delightful examples of Kashmiri craftsmanship.

Woodcarving

The Kashmiri woodcarvers are renowned throughout Asia, if not all over the world, for the fine detail of their workmanship, and examples will be seen everywhere – in shops, houses, souvenirs and, most glamorously, on the houseboats.

In the Kashmir Valley there seems to be a never-ending supply of walnut trees whose wood is ideal carving, being both hard yet malleable to knife and chisel. The natural veined surface of the wood and its variety of colour adds unique charm to finished pieces. Selecting the wood and maturing it for long enough for it to hold its carved features is an art learned from childhood among the woodcarving fraternity.

Visitors who stay on houseboats will see plenty of evidence of carved walnut as so many of the pieces of furniture in bedroom, dining-room or even up on the sun deck are either carved walnut, or teak.

The ceilings, too, will be intricately carved in patterns that are dizzyingly complicated. This is called 'pinjara' work. This wood is likely to be one of the local softwoods such as pine or budlu wood. The ceilings are not assembled by gluing pieces together; each piece is made to fit into its adjoining one by an ingenious and painstaking method of flanging. Geometric patterns are called 'khatamband' and are mostly made of pinewood slips which fit into each other. There are few houseboats, and mainland houses, which do not have some of these ceilings. Walls and screens are also a popular carved feature and serve to separate rooms or decorate around inside and outside windows. There are a bewildering variety of examples of this intricate work to be seen in the old British Residency, now a Government Arts Emporium.

One should beware of items which purport to be sandalwood as, unless it is a very small piece, it will be unlikely to be genuine and even then it could be suspect. Sandalwood is so expensive that any authentic piece, anywhere in India, would be costly. The supply of sandalwood and sandalwood oil is under Government control and, because of the tree's protection, is a rare commodity. Poaching is rife throughout India and whole trees disappear in the night from forest and estate and are soon sold either for export or to middle-men who sell again to the wood trade. In

Examples of expensive silverware

cheap boxes, for instance, that are sold as 'sandalwood', sandalwood slips are placed inside so as to give a scent of the real thing, and carved gods, for example, are rubbed with sandalwood oil for the same reason.

If the type of wood is of no importance then look for detailed fine carving that satisfies your eye, for no matter how precious the wood it is the carving of it that will give lasting pleasure.

Silver

Silverware of all sorts is on sale at all souvenir shops, emporiums and from shikara punts that ply the lake and river waters. The smaller pieces such as jewellery, bracelets, anklets, brooches and small boxes for attar or pills are the stock in trade of most traders. 'Only look, don't buy' is a favourite expression of the lake traders and it is these who can be too persistent around your houseboat. They can be a real nuisance, if they are allowed to become so. If you can't jolly them along and shoo them away, and this takes some doing, then speak to either your houseboat-boy or to the actual owner of the houseboat, the man you pay the rent to, and insist that no water-traders annoy you *at any time*.

The array of silver things is staggering and apparently unlimited in variations. Braclets will be studded with some semi-precious stone like lapis lazuli or agate; boxes will have moss agates and cornelian and moonstones studded in their tops and sides; there will be necklaces of silver filigree inset with turquoise, and anklets with tiny bells dangling. Often good pieces are made of old silver Indian rupees. Some pieces are boiled in fruit juice to encourage the silver's whiteness. After this unusual treatment it is polished to a brightness that will all too soon disappear and need the usual attention of periodic cleaning. White metal is also brought up to this fine state and looks deceptively like silver. A reputable dealer will admit the difference and also there would be a much lower price for the white metal. It is popular with the poorer people who buy silver only for important occasions like marriages.

Cricket bats

There is a curious and lucrative craft that exists not for tourists but for Indians. On the way from Srinagar to Pampore on the right-hand side of the roadway is a small but successful example of what might be called 'family light industry'. Here is collected, cut and cured the willow wood that is eventually carved into cricket bats. The wood is first stacked criss-cross-fashion into columns for curing, and when ready is machined, carved and varnished, and then hung under wooden roofs to dry. After this, fancy transfers of brand names are added and the cricket bats are then ready for 'exporting' southwards to the hundreds of sales outlets throughout the huge cricket-mad sub-continent of India.

10 Flora and fauna

Trees

As one travels around India and up into the regions of Kashmir certain species of trees stand out familiarly, trees one reads about in books. The palm is an obvious one, being a reminder of southern seaside towns of Europe and of hot-houses around the world. The banyan is another, ubiquitous throughout India; its dull dark-green leaves on rather haphazard branches, which have aerial roots hanging from them, often give welcome shade by the roadside, especially in towns and cities.

Countryside planting is mostly for crop yield, the tamarind being a favourite, as is the coconut palm. In the country are to be seen the really old trees of India, but alas they are ill-treated by vandals seeking fire-wood, and, due to the constant despoilation that has been unchecked by authority, thousands of trees have grown mis-shapen and grotesque. The best specimens are to be found in the many botanical gardens around India, or on private estates or public parks – gardens such as the Shalimar Gardens on the shores of Lake Dal.

There are many exotic specimens of trees and those travellers who wish to know more details about them would be well advised to obtain a copy of *100 Beautiful Trees of India*, by Charles McCann. This is well illustrated in colour and is obtainable from the publisher's bookshop, Taraporevala, of Bombay.

Here are some of the trees that may be identified.

Blue-flowering jacaranda (April–June), scented like hyacinths and seen *en route* to Srinagar by road at this time.

Mango, pungently scented through mid-March to mid-April.

Frangipani, scented like vanilla ice-cream and seen around temples – hence its other name, the temple tree.

Bauhenia, tall and rounded, bears a profusion of sweetly-scented flowers that look like miniature orchids in mauves and purples; the flowers can be picked and dipped in batter and eaten as a rather exotic snack!

Cassia, or *Indian laburnam*, is, as its name suggests, hung with bright yellow racemes.

Silk cotton tree, tall and erect with angular, spoky branches of a greyish colour, is, when flowering, an exuberant sight. It is from the seed pods of this tree that capok is obtained.

Gliricidia is a smallish tree which flowers in February-time. The flowers are cream or pale pink and attract many nectar-eating birds, among which is the Golden Oriel.

Rain tree is a large spreading tree with black bark and pale green foliage and bears flowers which resemble the flame of old gas burners, feathery things which detach themselves and float down as seed.

Jerusalem thorn, also called *Parkinsonia*, after John Parkinson (1567–1650), a British herbalist, is unusual in that its trunk is smooth and green. It has pine-like leaves and bright yellow flowers, and thorns that can tear flesh and clothing with ease.

Water pistol tree, botanically known as *Spathodia*, has large vermillion flowers that hold water. When they fall children pick them up and squirt juice at each other.

Casurina, a wispy, leggy tree, grey-green in colour, is often seen planted as a field crop for selling for charcoal production, or along coastlines to stop erosion.

Neem tree is said to be the most useful tree to the majority of people in India and is planted everywhere. It is a large tree with dainty leaves and sweet-smelling flowers from January onwards. Its gum is used in Ayurvedic medicine as an antiseptic; its green twigs are used for cleaning the teeth; its oil is added to toothpaste; a wine is prepared from its bark, and its flowers, mixed in curry, add health-giving piquancy.

Tamarind, too, is a most useful tree, often planted in the middle of fields or at village track intersections to give shade for the field workers. Without the fruit of the tamarind Indian cooking would be lacking a cardinal ingredient – the lemony juice extracted from the seed-pod. The tamarind gets its name from the Persian 'Tamar-i-Hindi', which means 'Indian Date'. The husks of the seed-pods have been used as road surfacing and the seeds ground and made into jungle bread.

Many of these trees form the background to Kashmir and the Valley and along the road route to Srinagar from Jammu. The following trees are more frequently seen when travelling around the Kashmiri countryside.

Rhododendron is a large shrub or tree growing up to 12 m (40 ft) which flowers during late March to the end of May. Its red flowers are acid in taste and, curiously, are used by many hill people to make a chutney.

Poplars are tall thin trees, sparsely-leaved with grey-green round or pointed leaves which flutter in the breeze. Seen growing up tall from islands and reclaimed land.

Eucalyptus adapts well to water-logged situations. Grown along river bank and beside the lakes together with poplars and willows; its leaves rustle pleasantly in the night and shed in the air its distinctive odour.

Birch is valued for its bark, which it casts off in strips or shards and which is exported for tanning, paper-making and is used to line some varieties of hookah – the hubble-bubble pipe.

Sal trees are tall, well-foliated trees, usually surrounded by many saplings. Most of the old wooden railway sleepers were made from the sal tree. The flowers are insignificant and bloom in March.

Walnut – ubiquitous throughout Kashmir, its craggy growth and venerable look, plus its distinctive pod fruits, make it easily recognisable.

Chenar or *Chinar* (spelt either way) is perhaps the most written-about tree growing in Kashmir. It grows tall and full, having broad leaves and thick branches. Its botanical name is 'Platanus orientalis'. It is distinctive in that in October and November its leaves gradually turn from green, through yellow, to a deep maroon, red and orange, all the colours of fire, and it makes a splendid sight against the snows that, by then, cover the nearby mountains.

Ber is seen on the roads when travelling to Srinagar via Jammu. It is called 'Zizyphus jujuba', is very thorny, and its fruits are much loved by passers-by and villagers and are picked and sold at market. Its main season is in January when its branches, especially those high up out of reach, are bowed down with the gooseberry-like fruit. The Latin 'jujuba' gives the name 'jujube' for jelly-like sweets.

Sebesten is a moderate-sized tree with large round leaves, white flowers and white cherry-like fruit. It makes a sticky mess of the ground below. Its wood is used for boat building.

Jambhool is a kind of myrtle. These large evergreen trees, with their dense shady crowns, are venerated by Buddhists and are often planted near a temple as they are sacred to Lord Krishna. The flowers are cream and fragrant and the fruit a favourite of jackals and civets.

Persian lilac will grow to 12 m (40 ft) but can be, and is, controlled as a hedge. It has fern-like leaves with lilac flowers in profusion that are very

highly scented. Seen in gardens and by the wayside, its seeds are used to make brown beads. The tree is nick-named the Bead Tree.

Other Himalayan and Kashmiri trees include ones that need no description. They are *oak, yew, cedar*, all *conifers, cyprus* and fruit trees such as *cherry, peach* and *plum*, all of which are magnificently in blossom in May, as are the *apple* trees, many orchards of which line the road down into Srinagar from the airport.

Flowers

Flowers of all kinds grow in abundance in this fertile valley. One cannot visit Kashmir and not see flowers, be asked to buy flowers or find them arranged around your hotel room or, especially, on your houseboat. The flower-seller boats call early in the morning to offer a variety to houseboat owners who then decorate the sitting-room, dining-room and writing desk or coffee table.

The flowers are cultivated between other crops, such as melon, cabbage, onions etc. All the English summer flowers seem to appear at one time or another. In springtime, arguably the best time for blossom, boat-loads of yellow and blue iris, hydrangea, tuberoses, marigolds and roses float around the lake on long colourful boats that have been tightly packed with clay pots which contain the water flowers need.

Flax is a favourite bedding flower, blue or red, and the Shalimar Gardens will certainly have borders of this bright flower. Its seeds are used for making linseed oil.

Roses are everywhere, but none is more spectacular than the 'banksia' variety which climbs over old buildings or pergolas in a mass of creamy blossom.

Wild flowers to be seen when walking around the Kashmir area are daisies, wild violets, sorrel, ferns such as Harts Tongue, maidenhair and bachelor ferns, St John's wort – plants that can easily be missed because of looking around at the magnificent scenery. Certainly the wild strawberries will easily be missed, growing so close to the ground. They flower and fruit at the same time almost continuously.

Lotus, sacred to the Hindus as the throne of the Goddess Lakshmi, is to be seen everywhere on the waters of the lakes. Its roots and seeds are a popular food. The most common variety seen will be the rose-flowered, or sacred, lotus, and the white-flowered water lily. The large leaves are anchored to the bottom of the lake by a tube-like thick stem which ends in

Birch and pines among the snowy landscape

a long root system. The surface of the leaves is wax-like, causing droplets of water to resemble beads of mercury when the leaf is wobbled. The flowers open at sunrise and close at eveningtime. They are not picked for decoration, probably because they are revered and also because they do not last long or stay open. The roots are a readily-available table delicacy on houseboats or at the hotel, and the seed-pods are eaten by locals and dried and used for table decoration or for export to the West for flower arrangers, as they are quite dramatic-looking.

Cucumber plant will be seen climbing over houseboats or over doongas. It has matted green leaves and beautiful large yellow trumpets. Roof-top gardening is an ancient custom and any type of climbing plant is suitable, mostly of the gourd family, but many roofs have tomatoes growing on them.

Crocus grows around Pampore and on the banks of the Jehlum river, and produces saffron. The Kashmiri saffron is world-famous and expensive. Fields full of pale-blue sweet-smelling flowers, whose scent fills the air, can be seen quite near to Srinagar. There are masses of small beds planted in a rotary manner so that each patch has a rest for one season in three. The flowers have six stigma, three of which are yellow and three orange. Children and women-folk separate the stigmas, the red from the yellow (yellow being second-class). The saffron industry is State-owned and therefore controlled and aided. To go camping in a field nearby crocus beds when they are in flower is to experience a rare olfactory experience.

Shrubs

There are many shrubs growing throughout India that are found around the Mediterranean regions and therefore will be familiar, but because of the oriental, romantic and unusual background will seem more exotic.

Oleander, as a free-standing bush or as a hedge, has fragrant pink and white flowers. Parts of the plant are poisonous so that cattle and goats, for instance, do not eat it. Its hollow stems are used for fashioning hookah pipes.

Hibiscus needs little introduction, though in India many varieties will be seen of every colour imaginable. The flowers are large and hang like huge bells, with their pollen-laden tongues protruding. There are double ones resembling full-blown roses and exquisite single blooms in delicate pastel colours.

Camphire is a commonly-seen Indian shrub. Another name is henna – the name of the well-known copper-coloured dye used by Muslims, especially those who have made the pilgrimage, or Haj, to Mecca, and also as a haircolourant in the West. The colour comes from a paste made from the leaves of the camphire. It is a straggly, prickly plant which bears spires of creamy flowers which are very fragrant.

Yellow oleander is a variety of the more usual pink-white oleander. It is free-flowering, has the same leaf shape and is unmistakable. Its trumpet-like flowers have a faint fragrance.

Yellow elder is fragrant and has yellow foxglove-like flowers which hang in clusters. Its botanical name is 'tecoma'.

Ervatamia (or *tageri* in south India, and *tagar* in the north) is colloquially named the moonbeam plant. This evergreen bears a profusion of white, wax-like flowers, large or small according to variety. The scent is delicate, and women like to bind the buds in their hair. The shrub can be recognised by its dark-green foliage and dazzlingly white flowers, like stars, which show up especially in the moonlight. A perfumed oil is extracted from its wood, the wood being also burned as incense.

Climbing plants

In Kashmir, as in other parts of India, one simply cannot miss the presence of climbing plants, in great varieties, so some idea of the names and habits of these excellent plants will be gathered from the following list.

Antigonon, often called the *Sandwich Island Creeper*, is a climber which can be seen covering railway fences, trellises and even really large trees and can be trained over wires as an effective hedge plant. It throws out sprays of tiny white and pink flowers from the end of the monsoon season and has a second flowering in the wintertime, December through to February.

Beaumontia grandiflora is a large evergreen shrubby climber which is often called the *Nepal Trumpet Climber*. It has large lily-like flowers and from a distance looks rather like a rhododendron. It is a showy plant, is a native of India, and has spread all over the country. It flowers from November to March.

The bignonias include some of the most gorgeous flowering climbers to be seen in India. Yellow, purple or red, their tubular flowers agglomerate to mask all signs of leaves. They can be seen on walls or pergolas in private gardens and in botanical gardens. The most brilliant is the pyrostegia, named for its fire-coloured flowers.

Bougainvillea was originally a native of South America. It is the most spectacular and ubiquitously-planted climber in India, tolerating almost all conditions. There is a bewildering variety of named plants, but ones like *Mary Palmer*, a double-coloured, cerise-white plant with variegated leaves, is a firm favourite. Other varieties are: *Aida* – rose madder; *Jubilee* – terracotta-orange; *Maharajah of Mysore* – pale rose; *Golden Queen* – orange-yellow; *Princess Margaret Rose* – magenta rose, and, of course, *Mary Palmer*. Bougainvillea has only one thing lacking and that is scent.

Jacquemontia is a twining plant and a favourite for screening purposes as the growth is dense and the flowering season perpetual. The flowers are bell-shaped, of a beautiful ultramarine blue, with a white eye, and they are profuse.

Quisqualis indica is better known as *Rangoon Creeper*. This climber has tubular flowers which start white and turn gradually pink and then orange. It gives out a fresh scent similar to that of the lime tree blossom of Europe. The flowers are in incredible numbers, borne in trusses and set-off admirably by the mid-green foliage. The climber reaches to a considerable height and, whilst perfuming a garden the whole day long, it is at night that the perfume increases. It is never cloying, always refreshing and will make the hottest night seem cool.

There are others like the ipomea – the morning glory – and the jasmine, honeysuckle, rose and wisteria that are a part of the Kashmir scene. A special mention must be made, however, of the 'banksia' climbing roses that bloom in Kashmir during May and June. They form cream mountains of dense, scented flowers and are a memorable sight.

Birds

It is not possible to be in India for very long without noticing, either by sight or by song, the many birds on the ground, in the trees and in the air; they seem to be everywhere. Visible or hidden, they command attention – sometimes by their brilliant colouring, sometimes by their sheer size, and often, like starlings in England, by their number.

Birds in India are protected to an extent by the Hindu respect for life, and it could be because of this that they fear man less and are therefore easier to spot. Despite this respect, though, many thousands of birds are trapped by one method or other and are sold as caged birds – a very lucrative trade. Bird markets are noisy places full of captured song birds. There will be hundreds of parakeets, finches and hill mynas, even owls, which are considered mysterious and are used in magic ritual. A questionable aspect of these places is that you will see species which are difficult to see in the wild.

Here are some birds that you will most certainly see during a visit to Kashmir and India.

1 A houseboat

2 Woodcarving on verandah of houseboat

3 Lake view from houseboat verandah

4 Kashmiri wool rug — 400,000 knots per square metre

Egrets Perhaps the cattle egret is the first bird that will attract the attention of a visitor. This quite white and fairly large bird travels with cattle, often the buffalo, riding on its back or scuttling underneath, the bird seizing the insects started up by the animal's movements. These egrets are also seen roosting in rice fields and their pure whiteness stands out against the intense green of the young rice.

Vultures The Bengal vulture, seen throughout India, is as large as a peacock, as, too, is the King vulture. The former is mostly brown whilst the latter has a red neck and red legs. Vultures eat carrion and large gatherings collect at animal carcasses which, no matter how big, are devoured with incredible speed. Repulsive when grounded, vultures are most graceful in flight.

Eagles and kites There are numerous eagles to be seen; the tawny eagle, the crested serpent eagle, the short-toed eagle are only some of the names. They are often shy of man and inhabit somewhat inaccessible places. Easier to see is the kestrel, by small rivers and waterways or near the stony river beds all around Kashmir.

The Pariah kite is a large dark brown bird, nearly as big as a vulture, and often seen wheeling on air-currents. The Brahminy kite is large and beautiful in flight; it is chestnut-coloured with white markings and is seen over ports and islands and large waterways such as lakes.

Peacocks Gone are the days when this exotic bird was served as the main course, complete with tail feathers decorating the dish. It is now a protected species and is the National Bird of India (apart from which it is a holy bird in Hindu mythology). It is seen all over India either in the wild or as a part of ornamental gardens.

Red wattled lapwing A familiar member of the plover family, this bird is a common sight. Its call is said to resemble 'did-he-do-it?' as it shrieks and swoops over the water or field. It is the size of a partridge, has brown back feathers and is white below, has crimson wattles by each eye and has yellow legs.

Crow pheasant This is a handsome, proud and cruel bird. Larger than a crow, it eats the young of other birds. It has bright chestnut wings and flops innocently around the bottoms of hedges, pecking for insects, and looking for nests. It has cruel blood-red eyes.

Kingfishers These birds are common all over Kashmir and are to be seen darting into the waters around the houseboats and pulling out small fish. The most common is the small blue.

Barbet Grass-green with a crimson breast, yellow throat and green-blue underparts, this is a small bird which is difficult to spot but not difficult to hear. It is nicknamed the coppersmith bird because of its incessant call which resembles beating on copper.

Hoopoe   A fawn bird with black and white bars marking the wings, back and tail, it has a conspicuous crest on its head. Its bill is curved and long and is used for probing into lawns for leather jackets and other larvae.

Blue jay   One of the most gorgeous birds and the size of a pigeon, it is described by India's foremost ornithologist, Salim Ali, as being Oxford and Cambridge blue, an apt description. Its breast is a dusky pink colour. When it flies its wings form huge blue fans.

Green bee eater   This is a small bird and is most colourful; it perches on wires and flies off catching insects – and bees if there are any. It is bright green with a rufous head and a characteristic long pointed tail.

Black drongo   A small, crow-sized bird, jet black and slim, with a deeply forked tail, this is often seen perched on telephone wires.

Golden oriel   This is a largish, bright golden-yellow bird with black wings and tail. It is hard to see amongst the leaves as it is a shy bird but well worth watching for among the tops of the trees.

Mynas   These happy, squabbling birds are all over India. They move in noisy colonies, sometimes completely covering a grove or large tree preparatory to roosting for the night, similar to starlings.

There are many different species of myna: the pied myna, as the name suggests, is black and white; the Brahminy myna is pinkish and brown, but the most common seen has yellow eyes and legs and white flashes on a rufous body.

Red vented bulbul   This is a smokey-brown bird with a distinguishing red vent under the tail. It has a cheery crest and hops among the lower branches of shrubs looking for insects.

The list of birds to be seen is endless but some others that you might see are hornbills, finches, woodpeckers, yellow wagtails, buntings, red starts, weaver birds and sunbirds.

Finally, one must not forget the scarlet minivet, an arboreal bird the size of a blackbird which has pretty scarlet feathers and a sweet song. It spends the winter in Sri Lanka and breeds in the lower Himalayas, and is seen to advantage from April to July, in and around the Moghul Gardens, high up in the trees.

Water birds

White-eyed pochard really is a domestic duck, rufous black-brown and with handsome yellow eyes. It nests around Kashmir's waters, its only breeding locality in India, from May to June. There will be many chicks bobbing on the waters at this time.

Little grebe or dabchick is a dull water bird with no tail, sometimes seen among river reeds, and generally below the 1500 m (5000 ft) level.

Brahminy duck is an attractive orange-brown bird with a cream head. It is seen by river and lake, and nests high up in Ladakh and Tibet – its nearest nesting grounds in India – from April to June.

Mallard nests in Kashmir from May to June. It is very common and bred for the table, and since it is mostly vegetarian in diet, it has tasty flesh that is not 'fishy-tasting'. It is a fast flier and much sought by sportsmen, and is beautifully coloured – grey head, rufous back, white and blue flashes on wings and a black curled tail.

Indian moorhen is a slate-grey marsh bird with long legs and an ungainly walk. It nests from July to September.

Coot is a slate-black dumpy bird which is tailless. It cries like a trumpet at night and can be a nuisance.

Whiskered tern nests from June to September. Like all terns it is a great flier, and when at rest the tips of its wings project beyond its tail.

Birds shot as sport, after obtaining a licence, are snipe, woodcock, sand grouse, duck and teal, patridge, jungle fowl, snow cock and snow partridge, dove and pheasant. A licence can be obtained from the Chief Wild Life Warden, Tourist Reception Centre, Srinagar, and it is a compulsory requirement.

Wild life

There is an abundance of wild life in and around Jammu and Kashmir. Some visitors may like only to observe and others may like to stalk and shoot, and in this part of India there is plenty of provision for both activities.

The State of Jammu and Kashmir sustains about 50 species of animals and more than 300 species of birds, with Jammu, being to the south and therefore warmer in wintertime, having a different range of species from the area north around Srinagar and the lakes.

To protect the wild life of the region the Department of Wild Life Protection has established several game reserves, some in Jammu and others in Kashmir and yet others high up in the Ladakh and Leh regions. There are also three National Parks, two Bio-sphere reserves and 33 Wetland Wild Life Reserves. All these are controlled and managed by trained staff and they are regularly visited by naturalists, biologists, conservation-

Brown bear of the hills

ists and preservation societies, as well as a large number of tourists.

Among the species that are to be seen in these sanctuaries are wild yak, brown bear, wild ass, monal pheasant, bar-headed goose, grey heron, bearded vultures and many others.

Kashmir is on the migratory route of Siberian water migrant birds which rest for a while, or nest on the less harsh waters around lakes. Many of these migrant birds are the object of the sport of shooting during the Kashmir winter season and one wonders that this annual culling has not deterred the winter bird visitors.

The situation of some game reserves and sanctuaries is listed below. Kashmir: the Dachigam National Park, the Overa-Aru Reserve, the Overa Wild Life Sanctuary.

In Jammu: the Kishtwar High Altitude National Park, and the Wild Life Sanctuaries at Ram Nagar, Nandni, Trikuta and Surin Sar Mansar. In the Ladakh area there is the Hemis High Altitude National Park.

Two species that are interestingly different and can be spotted by climbers and trekkers are the wild yak and the musk deer. Both are hunted

River fishing

animals. The wild yak has been driven into the highest and nearly inaccessible regions, making a hunt a hazardous undertaking. All yak are sacred to Buddhists. The musk deer is found only upwards of 1500 m (5000 ft) and is very shy. It has many enemies including the fox and eagle and the snow-leopard, and it is hunted by man for its musk. Musk comes from a 'pod' beneath the animal's stomach skin, and is a form of oily jelly. It is not necessary to kill the animal, as the 'pod' can be extracted on capture. Musk is used in perfumes, as an aphrodisiac and in some places to alleviate pain. The Chinese take it dried, as snuff.

Fishing

For many keen anglers Kashmir is paradise, and to cater for these enthusiasts there are many organised trout beats and other arrangements for visitors. One can fish for brown trout in spring waters at a relatively low altitude or, by pre-arrangement, journey up to the snow-fed waters some 3600–4300 m (12–14,000 ft) high. The sensation of being up and away from what can be a crowded lakeside, and experiencing the tang in the nostrils of the chill air beneath the warm sunshine, will make up for any fish that 'got away'. Camping out with a guide, or a gillie, is a good idea, the gillie being payed by you, per day.

The fishing season commences on the first day of April and ends on the last day of September – these dates depending on weather conditions, so that they could be a fortnight out either end. It is essential, therefore, to check in New Delhi before finalising any plans.

Fishing licences must be obtained from the Directorate of Fisheries at the Tourist Reception Centre. For tourists, fishing is allowed on only 6 days of the week, not Sunday. Advance booking of any particular beat is advisable and can be made through the aforementioned Department.

Fishing tackle can be hired and should preferably be from recognised dealers as there are many touts who will loan out poor tackle and blame the hirer afterwards.

It must be noted that spinning is strictly prohibited – no spinning, rod or reel is allowed for trout fishing. Locations for *trout fishing* are: The Lidder, from Pahalgam, Mughal Maiden at Kishtawar, Neern at Bad Rwah, Madumati at Bandipora; at *spring fed waters*: Kokermarg, Verinag, Gangabal; at *high altitudes*: Kishen Sar, Vishan Sar, Sheerashar.

Recommended flies are: Alexandria, Butcher, Coachman, March Brown, Muddler, Nymph, Peacock, or Watsons and Fancy.

Rod and line fishing is allowed after a payment of a fee – this is to fish for carp. No live bait is allowed.

There are cogent reasons why Jammu and Kashmir impose these restrictions and necessary permissions; they are to avoid over-fishing, to exclude all but the enthusiast, and to keep the whole atmosphere of fishing around the State something special and unique.

11 Trekking and sport

Walking and hiking

There are many ways these activities can be enjoyed in Jammu and Kashmir. One can go either alone or with friends or with an organised group, either entirely on foot, as in the case of simple walking around local areas, or by partly using ponies for longer experiences.

A good walk would be to go right around Lake Dal, taking a packed lunch and stopping here and there to explore the hillsides and returning at sundown. A morning walk up Shankaracharaya Hill is a good steady climb for the middle-aged, with superb views from the top. For young or old this is a popular walk at any time of day as the views are always changing. At sunset it is glorious and again at night, when Srinagar glitters below as a pattern of lights. One should allow 2 hours from bottom to top without hurrying.

Some longer journeys will take several nights and accommodation can be booked at the Tourist Reception Centre, Srinagar, for huts or Dak bungalows or hotels *en route*. These longer hikes need organising well – and well in advance – taking into consideration weather reports, available via INSAT, India's weather satellite. Clothing appropriate to the area to be hiked is important, as is the provision of supplies.

For even a one day walk around slopes and hills, adequate preparation should be made; the sudden thunderstorm, for instance, which may come on late in the afternoon and cause the unprepared to shelter, possibly until after sundown, when a light raincoat would have seen them through the rain, is one thing. Another is to take a map of the area showing the tracks and roadways and where rivers and bridges are. Follow a marked trail and do not deviate from it; note your half-mark time – it will take as long if not longer to make the return journey.

Remember you will be starting at an altitude of over 1500 m (5000 ft). Make provisions for rest stops and a break at the half-way mark. Take enough drinking water and some light food. Heavy spiced food induces

Easy walking round Gulmarg

tiredness, so it is better to take fruit, such as apples or bananas, or biscuits and sandwiches. Pack an antiseptic plaster or two, because a cut or blister can ruin the rest of a holiday if either become infected. Wear strong shoes even on what may seem a simple walk; shoes that tie are the best as they can be adjusted if the feet are getting tired.

One of the most interesting ways of going trekking is on a camping hike, by foot and on pony. For this it is usual to make arrangements to be away for at least two weeks in order to warrant the complicated equipment and guides etc. Preparations will include ponies, a guide, all food and water, and servants who will be ahead of you setting up camp for lunch or for the night. They will prepare all food, and the tent accommodation will be warm and comfortable. There is no experience quite like this and it is well worth considering and organising in advance; this can be done before arriving in India by contacting an agent or the Tourist Reception at Srinagar and remitting the necessary money in advance. If spending, say, a month in Kashmir, then these arrangements can be made on the spot. Payment will include everything except baksheesh – tips to porters and guide. It will be a less expensive holiday than it at first seems and is ideal for families.

In order to help plan hikes and treks and camping there follows a description of many that are possible. Plans can be made at the Tourist Reception Centre, Srinagar, and they will provide a local map as well as particular maps.

To protect the environment the local authorities expect certain rules to be observed:

> All refuse, *of any kind*, should be disposed of by burying.
> Keep to recognised tracks.
> Do not pick wild flowers.
> Only have *your guide* light a fire.
> Do not throw away cigarette ends – stamp them out.

Trekking around Kashmir

Jammu and Kashmir State offers a wide variety of trekking possibilities. The foothills of the Sawalik range of hills has many trekking routes and from the Kashmir Valley there are many alpine treks. Higher up, around Ladakh, are excellent opportunities for high-altitude trekking. Detailed information about various trekking itineraries are given in a folder entitled *Trekking in Kashmir and Ladakh*. The tourist department has published special trekking route maps which can be purchased from the Tourist Reception Centre, Srinagar, where, too, important equipment such as light mountain tents, sleeping bags, ruck-sacks and boots are available.

Trek 1	**Kolahoi Glacier**
Grade:	Easy
Maximum altitude:	3795 m (12,450 ft)
Time taken:	4 to 6 days
Most suitable time:	Mid-May to mid-October

A most gradual trek which does not involve the crossing of any pass. Built-up accommodation at two possible night-halts.

Day One: Srinagar–Pahalgam: 96 km (60 miles)
One can go from Srinagar to Pahalgam via regular bus, luxury bus or by taxi. Pahalgam is the setting-off point for many treks around the region. Here ponies can be hired, and porters too, and provisions such as tinned food can be bought.

Day Two: Pahalgam–Aru: 11 km (7 miles)
The road follows the Lidder stream with beautiful views of conifer-clad hillsides and the Tuliyan peak above Pahalgam. Aru is a small village situated at the end of a meadow through which runs a stream. Accommodation will be available at hotel, rest home, guest house and the tourist bungalow. A winter sports institute is planned at Aru.

Day Three: Aru–Lidderwatt: 11 km (7 miles)
There is an ascent of roughly 152 m (500 ft) immediately after leaving Aru, after which the trail has only gradual undulations. The distance can easily be covered in three hours. Lidderwatt, at 3000 m (9840 ft), is a small meadow with a river on two sides. Before reaching the meadow one has to cross the stream coming from the Kolahoi glacier. There is plenty of camping ground and plenty of drinking water. Apart from one's tent there is accommodation at a Public Works Department rest house and an alpine hut belonging to the Tourism Department. The views here are closed off by the depression in which Lidderwatt lies; one can, though, hike up the mountains and have fine views.

Day Four: Lidderwatt–Kolahoi Glacier and back
The track goes through a pine forest and, after some two hours, comes into the open at Satlanjan. A number of small streams have to be crossed by foot-bridges. There are shepherds' huts in the area for shelter. Half an hour after Satlanjan one can see the top of Kolahoi peak (5425 m [17,794 ft]). The track runs over boulders and scree to the foot of the glacier. The Kolahoi Peak is known as the Matterhorn of Kashmir. This is the site for the base camp for expeditions attempting to climb the peak. The return can be made in about three hours, the total day-long excursion taking from 6 to 8 hours, depending on diversions, and on one's pace.

Day Five: Lidderwatt–Tarsar: 12 km (7½ miles)
Starting along the stream to the east of Lidderwatt is the track that leads to the lakes of Tarsar and Marsar. The track runs through a forest and over boulders until reaching the mountain lake of Tarsar (3795 m [12,448 ft]). To reach Marsar one has to cross a ridge and make a descent and this can add a day onto the trek. The return trip to Tarsar Lake should take about 8 hours.

Day Six: Lidderwatt–Pahalgam: 11 km (7 miles)
A simple return, following the track, which will take about 5 hours. One can return to Srinagar the same day by setting off in good time.

Ponies, porters and tents can be arranged through the Tourist Office. There are fixed rates for various treks or excursions. Camping agencies

Amarnath Cave – the lingam of Lord Siva

hire out tents on a daily or weekly basis. Other items such as blankets, raincoats and cooking utensils are also available.

Pahalgam Club is a Government club which has, among other things, a roller skating rink, table tennis rooms and a card-playing room. Temporary membership is available.

Trek 2   **Amarnath Cave**
Grade: Moderate
Maximum altitude: 4218 m (13,835 ft)
Time taken: 4 to 6 days
Most suitable time: Mid-June to mid-October

Each year in July to August, at the full moon, thousands of pilgrims gather before the Amarnath Cave to offer their prayers to Lord Siva. Situated at a height of 3800 m (12,464 ft) in the Himalayas the cave enshrines a naturally-formed ice-lingam; the 'lingam' is the phallic symbol of Lord Siva. This ice formation waxes and wanes with the moon, reaching its maximum dimensions on the full-moon day of July–August. It is at this shrine that the Hindus believe Lord Siva explained the secret of eternal salvation to his consort, Parvati. Two of the God's servants overheard and were turned into pigeons and these, according to belief, can be seen flying away as the devoted pilgrims gather. Even at this time of the year at such a height the air is very cold indeed.

Day One: Srinagar–Pahalgam: 96 km (60 miles)
Drive from Srinagar to Pahalgam by taxi, coach or local bus. Stay in hotels, guest houses, etc. and arrange porters, ponies, tents, and whatever provisions may be needed.

Day Two: Pahalgam–Chandanwari: 10 km (6 miles)
The road is marked and is traversed by jeeps. There are beautiful views among the pines along the Lidder. Stay the night at a rest house. Water is available, especially for filling portable supplies.

Day Three: Chandanwari–Sheshnag: 12 km (7½ miles)
The next stage in the trek takes one to the emerald lake of Sheshnag (3718 m [12,195 ft]). The track follows the left bank of the Lidder for half an hour and then there is a tiring climb up the steep Pissu Ghati, at the top of which the track flattens out and goes right up to a gorge near the lake. To reach the lake it is necessary to descend quite a way. Many camp sites are available and plenty of water. Two-room rest houses and shelter sheds are there. Above the lake are the Trinity Peaks, and majestic glaciers. Very high winds blow in this area.

Day Four: Sheshnag–Panjtarni: 13 km (8 miles)
The track slowly climbs towards the highest point, Mahagunus Pass, and then descends through a long valley to a flat plain which was formed by the spreading out of two streams. After crossing this flat portion, Panjtarni (3657 m [11,995 ft]) is the next halting place where there are good camping facilities and where cooked food is available.

Day Five: Panjtarni–Amarnath Cave at Baltal: 19 km (12 miles)
Start early in the morning to trek up to the cave (3880 m [12,726 ft]). The track follows a narrow way and then descends to a stream coming from the Amarnath side. Follow this stream up to the cave. You will not be alone, for at any time during the visitable season there will be others making the same or similar journey.

On returning from the cave there is a steep climb and then a descent to Baltal. One can camp here for the night. If transport has been arranged one can drive straight to Srinagar.

Day Six: Baltal–Srinagar 94 km (58 miles)
From Baltal to Sonamarg is 8 k (5 miles), the first 5 on roadway of which the surface is rough, and the last 3 along the Leh highway – so often cut off in wintertime. One can either stay here or continue to Srinagar via the many local buses that are available.

Typical trekking scenery

Provisions, ponies, porters, dry rations etc. must be obtained at Pahalgam.

Trek 3	**Gangabal Lake**
Grade:	Moderate to difficult
Maximum altitude:	4081 m (13,385 ft)
Time taken:	7 days
Most suitable time:	Mid-June to mid-October

Day One: Srinagar–Sonamarg: 84 km (52 miles)
Sonamarg is a lovely mountain meadow surrounded by high peaks, and is at 2740 m (8987 ft), reached by a beautiful drive along the Sindh river. It is a fine permanent holiday place with many facilities and a good starting point for local walks.

Day Two: Sonamarg–Nichanai: 13 km (8 miles)
Return along the Sindh river to the steel bridge at Shitkari, after which the track goes north-west to Lashpatri. There is a gradual climb and then a steep portion until reaching some Gujar huts at a place called Shokdari, from where there are amazing panoramic views of the Sonamarg Valley, glaciers and mountain peaks. On through a birch forest, the track descends to a stream called Nichanai, eventually leading to the Nichanai Pass. Good camping facilities and drinking water are available.

Day Three: Nichanai–Vishensar: 12 km (7½ miles)
After crossing the Nichanai stream and, possibly, a snow bridge, the track climbs up the right side of the range to reach the Nichanai Pass itself (4080 m [13,382 ft]). There are many jagged peaks on the left side of the Pass. Descend and cross to a flat area where there are two beautiful mountain lakes, Vishansar and Krishansar, one blue and the other green, and with Mount Vishnu as a backdrop. The lakes are full of trout and a licence is needed for fishing. There are good camping grounds and in the summertime there are many shepherds grazing flocks of sheep and goats.

Day Four: Vishensar–Gadsar: 10 km (6 miles)
The track climbs up a steep pass, 4191 m (13,746 ft) high, on the right of Krishansar with Mount Vishnu to the left. After this pass, descend along the river to a small lake of deep blue colour which has, or might have, icebergs floating on it. The Valley then broadens out into a large plain, where there is another lake, known as Gadsar. All around this area grow a large variety of herbs and flowering plants.

Day Five: Gadsar–Satsar: 10 km (6 miles)
From Gadsar there are two possibilities. Immediately above the lake one can trek up the pass to descend straight to Satsar. The other route follows

the stream and goes round the mountain. At one point the stream disappears into a cave. Satsar consists of seven lakes set in a cascade formation, through the narrow valley.

Day Six: Satsar–Gangabal: 10 km (6 miles)
From Satsar the track descends along the stream and one should try to keep on the right of huge boulders, along the winding way to Zaji Mountain. One crosses Zajibal Gali (4081 m [13,385 ft]) to descend straight to Gangabal and there are dramatic views of Harmukh and other mountains. Gangabal, at 3570 m (11,710 ft) is a magical spot with streams full of fish, and beautiful mountain scenery, and it is worth spending two days just walking and climbing the area. There is the frequent thundering noise of breaking glaciers from the Harmukh mass.

Day Seven: Gangabal–Wangat: 16 km (10 miles)
Follow the stream down to Nundkol and onwards to Trunkhol. From this spot the track enters forest before reaching Naranag, where there are ruins of an old temple. Walk on to Wangat from where there are buses to Srinagar. The journey from Gangabal to Srinagar can be made in one day.

    Ponies, porters etc. can be arranged at Sonamarg. It is advisable to buy dry rations and anything special at Srinagar as there is little choice at Sonamarg.

Trek 4	**Lamayuru to Padham**
Grade:	Difficult
Maximum altitude:	5060 m (16,600 ft)
Time taken:	8 to 10 days
Most suitable time:	July to October

This trek is around the high regions of Ladakh and is mostly through high mountains completely barren of vegetation – greenery being limited to riversides, small valleys and wherever there is a sign of water. The climate is very dry, the days are hot and the nights very cold. In some places one may not find drinking water so it is better to go well prepared and fully equipped.

    Lamayuru is the oldest monastery in Ladakh and has a very majestic location on a hill overlooking ancient glaciers. It is situated on the Srinagar–Leh highway across the Fatu La Pass, which is the starting point for this popular trek.

    The route begins after making all arrangements and after arriving at Lamayuru.

Just one hazard

Day One: Lamayuru–Chila
A rough trek crossing the Wanla range (3245 m [10,644 ft]) for Chila, a small village and convenient stopover.

Day Two: Chila–Hanupata
To reach Hanupata one has to cross a very steep pass of 4265 m (13,990 ft) with lots of loose rock and scree on the trail. Water is a problem as the local river is saline! A fresh water well is located halfway up to Hanupata village; the village consists of a small group of houses and a gompa (monastery).

Day Three: Manupata–Photaksar
The route is good with a gradual ascent to Sirsir La at 4900 m (16,072 ft).

It will be over 10 km (6 miles) in distance, the village of Photaksar being surrounded by steep mountains. The area abounds with yaks. River crossing can be hazardous.

Day Four: Photaksar–Shanpado Gongma
Leave via a gradually-ascending trail to Singi La (5060 m [16,600 ft]). After some time there is a steep descent for about an hour before traversing the last pass and descending to Shanpado.

Day Five: Gongma–Linshat
The trail traverses along a mountain side gradually ascending to Linshat Gompa, which is one of the religious and cultural centres of the area. The gompa, or monastery, has about 60 lamas. There is a festival here held in July, around the 18th to the 20th. Some food may be available here but one should not rely on a supply.

Day Six: Linshat–Snertse
After the Pass of Hulum La at 4710 m (15,450 ft) the descent is through a wild valley with glacier and much snow. It is at the end of this valley that Snertse lies – a place where shepherds spend the summer.

Day Seven: Snertse–Pidmu
The trail fords a 4-m (13-ft) wide stream called Omachu and then descends into Zanskar Valley, through Hanumil. This whole day is easy walking.

Day Eight: Pidmu–Pishu
The trail runs up stream along Zanskar river via Zangla Gompa. There is a rope bridge across the river with a span of 130–150 m (426–492 ft) some 3 km (2 miles) before Pishu.

Day Nine: Pishu–Padam
The trail is easy now, following the river Zanskar upstream. It passes the village of Tongde where there is a large gompa. Padam is the end of quite a trek. The trek can be begun at the Padam end instead of at Lamayuru. It is advisable to take tents and good sleeping bags; villages *en route* have limited food supplies so all trekkers *must carry their own*, they cannot expect much help from locals.

Great caution must be exercised when crossing any river. During summertime these rivers are in spate due to rains and melt. One should try to cross rivers as early as possible in the mornings, when the waters will be at their lowest. *Never cross in late afternoon and never cross alone or without a rope anchor.*

There have been many accidents of drowning in this area and trekkers should take absolute precautions to prevent tragedies.

Ski bobbing

Water sports

On Lake Dal and Lake Nagin, during the summertime from July to September, *water-skiing* is very popular and, though the motor boats shatter the peace and churn the limpid waters, one has to accept this modern trend. The activity is usually a part of the facilities of one of the lakeside clubs.

Windsurfing, too, is gradually being seen more and more on the breezy waters, and what a blessing it is that this sport does not create noise; one of the great features of the Vale of Kashmir *used* to be its tranquility.

Swimming is everywhere and there are organised pools and areas set aside where swimming is safe from underwater reeds and currents. There can be very cold undercurrents and they can be quite strong-running too, so it is better to use the authorised places and not leap over the side of either the houseboat or the shikara punt.

River running is one of the more adventurous water sports – 'exhilarating and adventure-packed' according to local handouts. It takes place mainly high up in the Ladakh region on the Indus river and many of its tributaries which run through deep canyons and over long stretches of rapids. Inflatable rubber rafts are provided.

Winter sports

As soon as the first snows fall the valleys and highlands are transformed into a white world, a place that is quite unusual for winter sports enthusiasts as the surroundings are so dramatic. The country's main winter sports resort is Gulmarg, which has slopes varying between 2652 and 3200 m (8700 and 10,500 ft) with the highest ski runs in India. For the learner there are 3-week courses conducted by trained instructors of the Indian Institute of Skiing. There is also ski-bobbing. All this takes place over the highest golf course in the world which is then buried beneath deep snows.

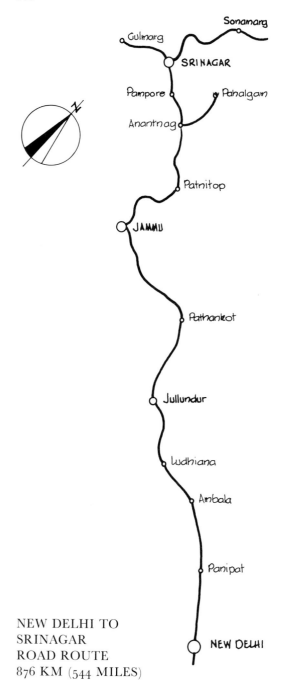

NEW DELHI TO
SRINAGAR
ROAD ROUTE
876 KM (544 MILES)

12 Jammu and environs

The environs of the city of Jammu are both fascinating and confusing. The old part of the city, with its bazaars and small hotels and mysterious courtyards, is set high above the bank of the river Tawi. From many vantage points there are splendid long views of the river with its temples and pavilions and, looking south, to the Plains of India.

The city is confusing in that there is little to indicate where the old and the new meet. This makes visitors very weary and often impatient because of getting wrong information concerning distances – few Indians have any real idea of distance – and exhausted too, because of the amount of to-ing and fro-ing necessary for getting around. The railway station, for instance, is beyond the old city and across a long bridge, several kilometres away from the old city.

Jammu is the gateway to Kashmir, and a part of the Plains, yet is rarely stayed at for more than a night or two, since visitors are eager to journey on to the Vale of Kashmir – especially so in summertime when Jammu becomes very hot and uncomfortable.

Little is known about this area before the eighteenth century AD. Legend relates that the city of Jammu was founded by one Raja Jambulochan some time in the early ninth century. The story goes that the Raja was out hunting when he saw a tiger and a goat drinking water together from the same pool. Considering this auspicious he decided to lay the foundations of a new city nearby. He named it Jammu Nagri – Jammu after his own name. Afterwards the city gradually became enlarged by means of trade and population; even so, there is scant writing about rulers before the Dogra Chief, Raja Dhru Deva, a Rajput who proclaimed himself ruler of the principality in AD 1730.

The Maharaja Ranjit Singh of the Punjab came to power later. His son, Gulab Singh, was granted a hereditary title of Raja in 1820, and in 1832 Raja Gulab Singh merged Jammu and Kashmir into one State under Dogra rule, which eventually acceded to the Indian Union in 1947, thus becoming a State within the newly-founded independent India.

The old city, as has been mentioned, bestrides the top of a hill overlooking the river Tawi. It is up here that the Tourist Offices and hotels are situated, and it is from here that 'luxury' coaches (luxury sometimes being sadly lacking) and bus tours set out. Down the hill is the General Bus Stand, or Station, from where buses can be used for a thousand and one local and long-distance journeys. If arriving by train, the only thing to do in order to get any trustworthy information is to travel over the bridge and up into the main, old city.

Most visitors use Jammu only as a transit place, but if time permits then to stop awhile and have a look round would not disappoint the curious. There are many excursions that can be arranged and help can be had from the hotel reception who will, in all likelihood, send a servant to book tickets and make any reservations necessary. This short stop-over should, ideally, be made no later than from the end of April through the first two weeks of May; after then is the perfect time to be arriving among the bustle of Srinagar and houseboats, and mountains.

Places of interest

Bahu Fort
Situated on a rock face 4 km ($2\frac{1}{2}$ miles) from Jammu, this is perhaps the oldest fort remaining in the area. Constructed by one Raja Bahulochan over 300 years ago, the site was later improved by the Dogra rulers. There is a temple dedicated to the goddess Kali inside the fort, and recently a beautiful garden has been laid out, complete with cafeteria.

Raghunath Temple
This is a city temple situated in the heart of the city. It is surrounded by many other temples and is in the Raghunath Bazaar.

Batote
At an altitude of 1560 m (5117 ft) this is a hill station some 113 km (70 miles) along the Jammu–Srinagar highway. Kud is a nearby hill village joined by bridle paths from which there are magnificent views. Accommodation can be found at Tourist Bungalows.

Mansar Lake
80 km (50 miles) from Jammu, Mansar is a small lake set in lovely surroundings; regular bus services run from the city. The trip is worth the effort for the scenery.

Patnitop
Situated 112 km (70 miles) from Jammu, Patnitop is a year-round resort, offering winter sports and summer picnics and holiday stays amidst breathtaking scenery; it is set high up on a plateau.

Vaishnodevi

This place attracts devotees from all over India for here is the shrine of Trikuta Bhagwati. Buses only go as far as a place called Katra, 48 km (30 miles) from Jammu; from Katra it is another 20 km ($12\frac{1}{2}$ miles) to the shrine, which must be covered by pony or on foot. The cave is reached by wading knee-deep through a stream. One does not have to go beyond Katra for interesting excursions, with many walks at the end.

Purmandal

39 km (24 miles) from Jammu, Purmandal is a place sacred to Hindus and a good picnic spot. Accommodation is sparse, being in pilgrim shelters, but return the same day is possible.

Amar Singh Palace

The tallest structure in Jammu, this palace towers above the river Tawi from its hilltop site. There are fine views over the city and its surroundings. It has been converted into a museum with a rare collection of Pahari paintings, family portraits of the royal family, and a library.

Dogra Art Gallery

This houses, among other things, a good collection of exquisite miniatures of the Pahari style. It is one place to make for in the city if time is short, and it is near the New Secretariat Building.

13 Srinagar and environs

The capital of Kashmir is Srinagar, a large city to the south of Lake Dal, which has a permanent population of close to 500,000. Through the city winds the river Jhelum which, before being controlled by canals and bridges and lock-gates, has been a part of the lake waters. Lake Dal is a beautiful spring-fed lake approximately 8 km (5 miles) long and 5 km (3 miles) wide, with islands and floating gardens, and houseboats. Peering down into the clear waters one can see the river current bending the reeds.

Srinagar is a crowded city, made up of noisy, fascinating bazaars, crossed by numerous waterways which bustle with shikaras, houseboats, doongas, on which whole families live, and all manner of traders, some of whom are dauntingly persistent. The place makes little sense until one has walked around for half a day and got one's bearings.

The majority of the people differ in their looks from the more familiar Indians of the Plain. Kashmiris have longish faces, large noses and are fair-skinned. Some are dashingly attractive and the women radiantly beautiful – a beauty often hidden by head shawl or burquah, a garment which covers up the whole body, with an eye-piece of lace or crochet-work. More of this adherence to tradition is to be seen as Islamic fundamentalism permeates the Muslim society.

The name Srinagar includes both the land city and that part that is around the waters, on islands and by river banks, and it is difficult to tell where water dwellings end and terra firma begins. The part of Srinagar that is an island, formed by the river Jhelum making a loop, has to its south an embankment called the Bund – one of the most frequented parts of the city. The main Post Office is on the Bund as are many of the famous craft emporiums. Nearby is the Tourist Reception Centre and the head-quarters of many tour operators. Nearby, also, is the old British Residency, now the Government Arts Emporium, and there are restaurants and every kind of souvenir shop.

The waters of lake, canal and river are controlled by dams or lock-gates, depending on the different levels of the lake and other waters. The Dal

Srinagar as it was some years ago

Gate lock is one such and much fun can be had watching the shikara boys waiting for the lock to fill and then being first out onto the canal. If you are actually on a shikara boat, waiting to proceed, you will undoubtedly be approached by numerous traders trying to sell you anything from a silver anklet to a Persian carpet.

Never far away in the city or on the waters is the sight of the distant mountains and foothills, and of Shankaracharaya Hill, with its Hindu temple on top and the television mast spoiling the view. All around are

Third bridge over River Jhelum – Srinagar

graceful willow trees dipping their leaves into the waters, their branches flowing with the currents and eucalyptus and poplar trees reaching to the blue sky.

When travelling on the water one passes all manner of watershops, such as a chemist, distinguished by a large red cross on its side, a flower seller, a potter's shed, a woodcarving workshop. Many of these shops will be built on piles driven down into the mud close to the bank of an island and will have a small landing stage with water-logged wooden steps leading upwards. In among these shops are houseboats and bungalow-type houses, built of brick and wood in the hill-station style, and the occasional hotel will appear through the trees. Much water-land has proved firm enough to hold the foundations of quite large buildings, built high up enough to avoid being flooded when the huge amount of snow melts from March–April onwards.

The floating vegetable market on Lake Dal

An interesting trip before breakfast, at about 6am, is to go via your shikara to see the floating vegetable market, where many long punts gather laden with all sorts of vegetables: cabbage, kohlrabi, carrots, gourds, tomatoes etc. You will see women manoeuvre their boats and trade and buy from the water dealer for the kitchens of both houseboat and cook-boats and for private needs. There will be a mist over the water like a thin veil and the air will be silent and cool. It is, by the way, an excellent time for photographing the mood of the lake, giving some unusual effects.

Later in the day, men will be 'poling' – plunging a pronged pole into the waters where the lotus roots grow; lotus root is called 'nadru' and is much used as a vegetable. One could order it cooked in a white sauce with casserolled duck and be pleasantly delighted at its flavour. Avoid roast duck as this has the greatest chance of being served tough, whereas casserolling at least will make sure the meat is tender.

When out on the water in your shikara ask your shikara-boy to find you some honey. Kashmir honey is famous; it is found locally and gathered wild, and it is the wild that has the best flavour.

Also out on the water observe the floating gardens. They are a unique feature of Kashmir and are made of matted reeds to about 60 cm (2 ft) thick in depth and to any size that is required and can be towed to any desirable position and fixed by poles driven into the lake bottom. On top of these floating gardens are piled mud and weed which have been dredged from the lake bottom. Before planting, the patch is manured, and then set with crops such as brinjal (aubergine) or marrow, pumpkin and cucumbers, cauliflowers and peas, and this floating garden needs no watering! It can be moved lock stock and barrel if the need arises, when the securing poles are lifted and the whole growing island moves, guided by punts on either side. Moving is usually only caused by a drought or if the lake water level lowers. The constant hooking up of weed from the lake bottom ensures that the water is free from pollution, clean and easily navigable.

When on the water watch for the dragonflies. There are a great variety and they flit incessantly around among the reeds and the houseboats. Very flashy are the ruby-red ones which tend to hover close to the water's surface and then dart away, probably alarmed by a kingfisher or a darting swallow.

As darkness descends the lake becomes quiet and like a mirror so that the stars join the many lanterns and porch lights of the houseboats, and fireflies float around amongst the willows. In the distance will be heard the last of the many 'muezzins' chanting prayers from the minarets of surrounding mosques.

A sultry afternoon, shikara passing houseboats

These sights and sounds, and the keen mountain air with its scent of flowers and pine-wood and log fires, are what contribute to the magic of Kashmir and, together with its people, make it unique.

Places of interest

Chashmashahi Gardens

This is a pleasantly laid out garden in terraces with a spring of icy-cool water, originally designed by the Emperor Shah Jehan in AD 1632. Part of this area has been laid out as a tourist village. The gardens are illuminated at night, and day and night offer magnificent views over the lake and city of Srinagar.

Lake Dal

This local and extensive lake is divided by causeways into four parts: Gagribal, Lokutdal, Boddal and Nagin. Lokutdal and Boddal each have an island in the centre, called Rup Lank and Sona Lank respectively. Rup Lank is another name for the small island on which there are four chenar trees and a small pavilion, called the Char Chenar island, because of the four chenar trees.

Hari Parbat Fort

This fort is visible from almost anywhere on the lake. It is 5 km (3 miles) from Srinagar to the north east. The fort is surrounded by trees and scrub and was constructed by Mohammed Khan, an Afghan Governor of the province, in AD 1592–98. There are almond blossom trees blooming in the spring. Permission to visit must be obtained from the Director of Tourism.

Harwan

Near to the Shalimar Gardens is this village in which there are interesting remains of ancient ornamented brick pavements of the early Buddhist period. The tiles show the dresses of the people, such as Turkoman caps, large ear-rings, loose trousers and close-fitting turbans, all showing a central Asian influence.

Hazratbal

Situated on the western shore of Lake Dal, this Muslim shrine has a special sanctity containing, as it does, a sacred hair of the Prophet Mohammed. This relic is displayed to the public on special occasions. Hazratbal lies opposite the Nishat Garden over the waters. It is a village of higgledy-piggledy houses all of which, in the springtime, seem to be abounding with new life – ducks and chickens and puppies and kittens, as well as human babies!

Jamma Masjid

Originally built by Sultan Sikandar in AD 1400 this mosque was later enlarged by his son, Zain-ul-Abdin. It is finished in Indo-Saracenic style, much of which has been destroyed by fire but re-built each of the three times this misfortune happened until the present form was repaired during the reign of the Dogra Maharaja Partap Singh.

Nishat Bagh

Over on the banks of Lake Dal, 11 km (7 miles) from Srinagar, with the Zabarwan mountains at the back, this garden has fine views of the lake and, in the distance, of Hari Parbat Fort. Beyond is the snow-capped Pir Panjal mountain range. The garden was designed by one Asaf Khan, brother of the wife of the Emperor Jehangir, Nur Jahan, in AD 1633.

Lake Nagin
Referred to as 'The Jewel in the Ring', Lake Nagin is the smallest of the lakes but is perhaps the most lovely. It is separated from the main Lake Dal by a causeway over which one can walk to Hazratbal. Its waters are a deep blue and it is surrounded by a circle of green trees, hence its name. There is a club on its shore with facilities such as water skiing and swimming. This was once the quietest of places and still is in the springtime, but in summer its tranquility is shattered by speedboats and transistors.

Pari Mahal
This was once a Buddhist monastery but was converted into a School of Astrology by the Emperor Shah Jehan's son, Dara Shakoh. It is situated on a spur of mountain overlooking Lake Dal and has well-kept spacious gardens and is an ideal picnic place with walks around onto the surrounding hillsides. It is near the Chashmashahi Garden to which it is connected by a small roadway. It is well-lit at night and the whole place is illuminated during the early evening.

Pather Masjid
This stone mosque is in the heart of the city, opposite the Shah Hamdan Mosque. It was built by Nur Jahan and was then mainly reserved for the prayers of the Shia Muslims.

Shah Hamdan Mosque
This is one of the oldest mosques in the city and is situated on the banks of the river Jhelum. One can approach either by road or by water. There are walls lined with beautiful papier-mâché work.

Shalimar Gardens
Built by the Emperor Jehangir for his wife, Nur Jahan, this is a beautiful garden, steeped in history and legend and song. One thinks of 'Pale Hands I Loved Beside the Shalimar', a famous Victorian parlour and concert song. The garden is wide and deep and has four terraces rising one above the other. A canal runs through the middle supplied with water from a stream running from the mountains behind. There is a Sound and Light Show run by the Indian Tourism Development Corporation during May to October.

Shankaracharya Temple
On the top of a hill having the same name, it rises 300 m (1000 ft) above Lake Dal and dominates the surroundings. This Hindu temple goes back to the times of the Emperor Ashoka, around 200 BC. The present structure is thought to have been built by an unknown Hindu devotee during the tolerant reign of the Emperor Jehangir. The hill is also known as Takht-i-

Achabal Garden

Sulaiman. An early morning climb is most rewarding – the best time, before breakfast, to see the sunrise.

For general information about the Moghul Gardens see p. 75.

There are many excursions that can be taken from Srinagar and booked at the Tourist Reception Centre. Some of them are listed below, in alphabetical order. A sequential order is given at the end.

Achabal

A fine garden at an altitude of 1677 m (5500 ft), it was designed in the Moghul style with groves of trees, water cascades and fountains. This was once a pleasure retreat of the Empress Nur Jahan. There is a camping ground here and a trout hatchery. It is 58 km (36 miles) from Srinagar. Half way there is Avantipur where there are ruined temples believed to have been built by Avanti Verman in the ninth century in honour of the

5 A brightly-painted shikara visiting houseboats with the Himalayas
in the background

6 Gulmarg, the circular walk; Pir Panjal mountains in the distance

7 The road to Gulmarg

8 Food stall *en route* to Srinagar

god Mahadeva. There is a refreshment cafeteria here and accommodation at a Tourist Bungalow and Tourist Huts.

Aharbal

This is a favourite place for Indian visitors, 51 km (32 miles) from Srinagar. The huge and impressive waterfall is formed by the river Veshav falling from a height of 25 m (82 ft). 11 km (7 miles) onwards is Kounsernag Lake, which usually remains frozen and covered by ice flows until late June. This whole area is a walker's and trekker's paradise. There is accommodation at a Tourist Bungalow and a PWD Rest House.

Burzahom

Some time ago excavations here revealed settlements dating back to 2500 BC. It is 24 km (15 miles) from Srinagar by bus and there is fine walking all around.

Charari-Sharif

30 km (19 miles) on the road to Yusmarg, in the hills of the Pir Panjal range, is the ziarat, or shrine, of the patron saint of Kashmir, Sheikh Noor-ud-Din, more popularly known as Nunda Rishi.

Dachigam National Park

Originally a royal game reserve, this sanctuary is now a protected area and provides shelter for various species of wild animal, such as the Himalayan black bear, the brown bear, the musk deer and the hangul, or Kashmir stag. Tourists are required to obtain special permits to visit here, available from the Chief Wild Life Warden at the Tourist Reception Centre, Srinagar. It is 21 km (13 miles) from Srinagar.

Daksum

This is a peaceful unspoilt forest retreat encircled by mountains, situated 85 km (53 miles) from Srinagar and at a height of 2438 m (7996 ft). There are regular bus services. A cafeteria provides meals and there is a Tourist Bungalow. If walking, one can cross from here over the Simthan Pass to Kishtwar in Jammu, from where one would need to get a long-distance bus back.

Ganderbal

There is excellent camping here, on the banks of the river Sindh with shade from tall chenar trees. It is only 19 km (12 miles) from Srinagar, and so one could hire a bicycle and go that way.

Kokarnag

This is famous for the curative properties of its springwater, and there is a botanical garden which specialises in growing roses. Food can be obtained here and there is accommodation in Tourist Bungalow and Tourist Huts. Accommodation should be reserved, as many Indian tourists visit here to take the waters.

Manasbal

This lake is on the circular walk from Lake Dal around Lake Wular – quite a long walk incidentally. Manasbal is a bird watcher's paradise. It is 32 km (20 miles) from Srinagar and Tourist Bungalows are available.

Martand

There is a spring here that is very sacred to the Hindus; it is a place of pilgrimage. It is 60 km (37 miles) on the Pahalgam road. There is dormitory accommodation, and it is a beautiful place for back-pack walkers.

Pampore

This is a famous plateau over which is grown saffron, for which Kashmir is famous. Fields and fields of crocus bloom pale mauve and scent the air. The stamens are plucked and dried here.

Sonamarg

Literally 'the meadow of gold', Sonamarg is up in the wild mountain ranges, 2740 m (8987 ft) high, and is a fine base from which to walk the surrounding area. There is a rest house here and other accommodation.

Thajiwas

Only 4 km (2½ miles) on from Sonamarg, this is a small valley at the foot of the Sonamarg glacier. Here there are alpine huts and a forest rest house.

Verinag

There is a spring that rises here that is reputed to be the chief source of the river Jhelum. There are remains of a pavilion and baths built during the Moghul period. It is 80 km (50 miles) from Srinagar and one can stay the night at either a Tourist Bungalow or Hut.

Lake Wular

This is a great fresh-water lake, the largest lake in India, and is an important hydrographic feature which controls the waters of Kashmir. It acts as a reservoir and takes any excess flood waters, consequently its dimensions differ during the year. Normally it is 19 km (12 miles) long by 10 km (6 miles) wide. This lake is surrounded by mountains and is attractive in a grand way, unlike the smaller lakes which have a more intimate charm.

Yusmarg

40 km (25 miles) from Srinagar, this is a small open valley in the hills of the Pir Panjal range. Giant pines and firs cover slopes on either side. Ponies are

available for trips to nearby places and there is accommodation available. One should reserve this in advance before leaving Srinagar.

It is useful to note the sequence of these places as, if touring by car, arrangements can be made for accommodation. Pampore, Avantipur, Anantnag, Achabal, Kokarnag, Daksum, Martand and Veringa are all in a line from Srinagar.

Pahalgam

Situated at the junction of the Lidder and Sheshnag streams, Pahalgam has been a camping and trekking ground for years in the summertime. It is 610 m (2000 ft) higher than Srinagar, set in a wood of blue pines with clear fresh pine-scented air. It was originally a small village of shepherds which has gradually grown into a hill resort. There are good walks locally and good fishing for those who have the necessary permit. Pahalgam is also the base for making a pilgrimage to the sacred cave of Amarnath. It is 96 km (60 miles) from Srinagar. The cave of Amarnath is 66 km (41 miles) farther on and is about 3962 m (13,000 ft) above sea level, above all vegetation such as trees and shrubs, set amongst wild and impressive scenery.

Amarnath

As mentioned, 66 km (41 miles) from Pahalgam, Amarnath is a 3 to 5 day trek (see section on *trekking*, p. 107). The route goes via Chandanwari, 16 km (10 miles), and then via Sheshang and Panchtarni. One can make the whole distance by pony and porters, or by pony with friends. One should not go alone, but there will undoubtedly be Hindu pilgrims making their way there, especially in the months of July and August – the auspicious time of that month's full moon being the main pilgrimage time for Amarnath.

Baisaran

Only a couple of kilometres from the bazaars of Pahalgam, and signposted, Baisaran is a glen in the pine and fir forests, commanding a fine view of the valley. It is about 150 m (492 ft) up the mountainside.

Kolohoi Glacier

This is a three-day trek, the path winding through woods to the meadow of Aru, where one can camp for the night, going on to Lidderwatt, 11 km (7 miles), to another camping ground set in a meadow surrounded by dense forest. From here it is another 13 km (8 miles) on to the Kolohoi Glacier.

Mamlesvara

Just 1.5 km (1 mile) down from the bridge at Kolohoi there is a small ancient stone temple consecrated to Siva Mamlesvara. The temple was built before the twelfth century. There is, too, a picturesque stone-lined water tank. This whole area is strewn with wild flowers like primulas, cranes bill and gentian.

Tarsar Lake

13 km (8 miles) from Lidderwatt, or 35 km (22 miles) from Pahalgam via Aru, there are delightful camping grounds at a place called Sekiwas, 2 km (1¼ miles) from the lake, surrounded by flower meadows. The air can be chilly up here, even in the summer.

The season up in these hills is from mid-April to mid-October, and the recommended clothing is light woollens for summertime and heavy woollens for wintertime, though it is better to take a mixture as mountain temperatures can be capricious.

Gulmarg

This is one of the most interesting, charming and easily accessible places near Srinagar. The word Gulmarg means 'meadow of flowers', and this is an apt description. Originally named Gaurimarg, in honour of Gauri, one of the names of Lord Siva's wife, its name was changed in 1581 by King Yusaf Shah, a regular summer visitor. In 1908, Sir Francis Younghusband in his book *Kashmir* predicted 'what will be one day known as the playground of India. . .'; and his prediction has become true, for this area of Kashmir has become world-famous both for winter sports and for summer walking. It also has the highest golf course in the world.

The main charm and glory of Gulmarg, though, is its scenery and the views of the great peak, Nanga Parbat, 8000 m (26,260 ft) above sea level. The meadow itself is saucer-shaped, over which traverses the golf course and around which runs a circular walk lined with spruce and blue pine, maple and chestnuts, among which have been built vantage points and picnic spots where walkers can sit and gaze with wonder at the mighty Nanga Parbat and the whole range of the Himalayas. This track is quite

Tobogganing with servants, Gulmarg

level and presents no difficulty for walkers. Should you arrive there too
early in the season then special walking over-boots are loaned to protect
from snow, ice and slush. In the distance can be seen Lake Wular and the
glinting roofs of the temples, mosques and bazaars of Srinagar.

Gulmarg is an excellent winter sports centre and a fine base from which
to go trekking. It is 56 km (35 miles) from Srinagar, accessible by road or
by the public bus which stops at Tangmarg, from where one can either

Gulmarg golf course

walk the distance to the top or engage a pony from one of hundreds that will be waiting.

The 18-hole golf course here has recently been relaid to international standards. It is described in the brochures as the highest green golf course in the world. To play there is certainly a stimulating experience and the views are magnificent. Golfing equipment is scarce so it is advisable to take your own.

The Srinagar to Tangmarg road passes through many rice fields and poplar avenues, gradually rising until it winds towards Tangmarg into pine forest and over gorges and mini-glaciers.

At 2653 m (8702 ft) above sea level, Gulmarg is the only ski resort in the Himalayas. The skiing season operates from 15 December through to 15 April. There are many opportunities for cross-country skiing and ski-mountaineering. Trained instructors are on hand and short ski courses can be arranged, usually of three weeks' duration on an all-inclusive basis.

There are ski lifts and tobogganing and ski-bobbing; there are also T-

Khilanmarg, with glorious views of the Vale of Kashmir

bar ski lifts and ski-lifts with chairs. Both adults and children are catered for at every level.

Treks from Gulmarg

Alpather Lake (13 km [8 miles])
At the foot of the main Apharwat peak and behind a ridge are the ice waters of this far-away lake, which remains frozen until the middle of June. One can go by pony there and back.

Banibali Nag
This is a small lake formed by landslides above Ferozepur stream and 5 hours' journey from Gulmarg. This is really a day's outing, leaving early and going by pony.

Khilanmarg
Only a 40-minute uphill walk from Gulmarg, this whole area is carpeted with flowers. There are unrivalled views of Lake Wular, other lakes, and

the surrounding peaks. A must for any visitor to this charming part, this is an easy walk and a marvellous place for a day out, taking a picnic.

Ziarat of Babareshi

This Muslim shrine is 5 km (3 miles) from the middle gap to the east of the Gulmarg Valley; the path leads down through thick forest. The ziarat, or tomb, is that of Baba Payam-u-Din, a revered Muslim saint who lived here during the Moghul rule. Interestingly, both Muslims and Hindus make offerings and say prayers here.

14 Ladakh

Advice and regulations

Always carry a protective cream or gel for face and hands to save them from sun burn. Carry, also, a plaster, some aspirins, water purifying tablets, travel sickness tablets and medicine for stomach ailments. If there are serious symptoms of illness then consult a doctor.

Respect the religious sanctity of all monasteries – these are part of the Buddhist religion and culture. Do not drink or smoke in a monastery. Remove your shoes before entering a monastery or any of its outbuildings. Do not touch statues or thankas or the silver-plated surfaces of the chortens inside a gompa, or monastery.

Do not use photo-flash inside a monastery, the light-charge will damage the colours of the delicate frescoes. Do not try to insist on accommodation in a monastery; they have the absolute right to refuse accommodation, without giving a reason.

Do not buy objects which are more than 100 years old as these are defined as antiques and their sale *and their purchase* is prohibited under law.

Carrying local apples, fresh apricots, fresh walnuts and any of their saplings out of Ladakh is banned under local laws; proper permission must be obtained.

Do not take photographs of bridges, strategic locations, i.e. near border territory, around military camps and such installations, as this is *strictly prohibited*.

The region

Ladakh is a frontier district of northern India, often referred to as 'Little Tibet'. It is the highest region in India, comprising gigantic mountain

Young Ladakhi girl

ranges interrupted by deep and narrow valleys. The area is made up of Ladakh to the east and Kargil and Skardu, sometimes referred to as Baltistan, to the west, the whole area formerly being the most westerly part of Tibet. Ladakh lies between the Karakoram range and the eastern Himalayas, in a valley of the upper Indus. The Ladakhi people are correctly Tibetans and are Buddhists, whilst the inhabitants of the Kargil region are mainly Shia Muslims, Islam being introduced – imposed may be a more appropriate term – to these peoples in the sixteenth century AD by missionaries. These people are called Aghas locally, and they keep their faith alive notwithstanding being surrounded by ancient folk traditions of their ancestors which are imbued with a mixture of animism and the later Buddhism. The capital of the whole district is Leh.

Ladakh is a land of unsurpassed mountain beauty, of fascinating monasteries, and has, on the whole, an arid and harsh climate. Here live such rare animals as the highland yak and the kiang, or Tibetan wild ass.

Leh

The capital city, Leh, is situated at one of the junctions on the famous 'silk route', which started from Sinkiang in China to western Asia and into the plains of India. Leh is 3500 m (11,480 ft) above sea level, is a military base and, therefore, is a sensitive area, and one is not allowed more than 1.6 km (1 mile) north of the Srinagar–Leh road. The city lies some 10 km (6 miles) north-east of the Indus. In reality it is more a town, and is made up of small lanes and alley-ways, intermingled like jigsaw pieces, over which the Leh Khar Palace stands guard.

This palace was built in the sixteenth century by Sovang Namgyal and inside are old wall paintings depicting the life of Buddha, as well as painted scrolls, statues and armaments. It is known as the Leh Museum. In the main bazaar stands the Leh Mosque, built in AD 1594 by Singe Namgyal as a tribute to his Muslim mother; this mosque is in the Turko–Iranian style with exquisite carvings of pillars and screens. Nearby is the Tsemo Gompa, one of the royal monasteries, which is known for its huge two-storied statue of Buddha in the sitting posture. Towering over all is the Leh Monastery, built high up on huge crags, dominating the town. It houses painted scrolls and ancient manuscripts and wall paintings, but its main treasure is the solid gold statue of Lord Buddha.

To reach Leh by road one has to travel 434 km (270 miles) along the Srinagar–Leh highway, following the old trade route. The scenery all the way is magnificent, passing unknown villages, through gorges and over the famous ZojiLa Pass. One might say of this pass that it is infamous in that it regularly claims lives because of avalanches. As recently as October–November 1986, 65 vehicles were suddenly trapped in snow drifts that happened too quickly for escape; many lives were lost. In the summertime, though, this pass is innocently benign, yet it is no less dramatic, with incredible views over Kargil, and its surrounding cultivated fields contrasting with the barren mountains.

Ladakh's climate is one of sharp contrasts, contrasts that make its unique beauty shine in the summer sun beneath azure skies. Below are

Polo playing at Leh

desolate rocks, unapproachable mountains and tempting green pockets of arable land near to perched monastic buildings. Many of these buildings are extensive, being added to over the years in a rather haphazard way so that they spread over quite a large area.

Monasteries

An emissary of the Emperor Ashoka was responsible for the birth of Buddhism in Ladakh. This began with a gradual rejection of idol worship replaced by the veneration of Lord Buddha in symbolic form – either as a statue or in murals or paintings. There is much of this ancient evidence of Buddhism to be seen in all the monasteries in Ladakh, called gompas.

The spiritual life of Ladakh centres around these glorious monasteries which are places of worship, a home for the dedicated monks who tend them; they have served throughout the years as a place of refuge and temporary residence for thousands of itinerant traders who have passed through this sparse region.

Ladakh has twelve main monasteries, most of which can be visited by bus from Leh. The time one should pay a visit is between the hours of *6am*

Tibetan prayer wheels and prayer caskets

and 9am. There will be an entrance fee which may or may not be included in an organised tour.

Each of the monasteries has some very high buildings, floor on top of floor, which make them conspicuous from afar. The path leading to them is usually lined with smallish metal cylinders, called 'chhoskor', meaning prayer wheel. These cylinders are filled with prayers and charms. Before entering the monastery a devotee will set a cylinder in motion by gently stroking it, and the belief is that he will be sending up prayers to heaven equal to the number in the cylinder and multiplied by the number of rotations.

There are several tour operators in New Delhi, Bombay and in the West who arrange visits to this area, either in order to trek or to mountaineer or just to go as a tourist as part of a holiday in Kashmir.

Indian Airlines fly up to Leh from Srinagar cutting the journey time to little over a half an hour. One has to be aware, though, of the many difficulties that flying entails. The weather is the greatest bogey as it can

Typical hill people

change even during flight, and planes that have taken off at Srinagar may not be able to land at Leh or vice versa. There are, consequently, many delays, especially early in the season, and these can disarrange a whole itinerary. Early in the season, too, because the roads are cut off, flights will be over-booked. Really one should arrange to visit Ladakh only during the summer season, from July to September, so that the journey has a reasonable chance of being smooth and the weather up in the mountains warm. As the air up there is rare the sun can be very harmful and will burn the face and hands quickly. A sun screen cream should be used. Also, should there be a slight clouding-over, the temperature will drop radically in minutes – therefore tie a woollen around the waist.

Hemis Gompa

This is Ladakh's largest monastery, 49 km (30 miles) from Leh on the Manali road. The monastery contains several gold statues and stupas decorated with precious stones and has a superb collection of thankas including one which is reputed to be the largest in the world and is exhibited only once every twelve years, the next time being in 1992. Colourful flags flutter on the four pillars in the main courtyard against the brilliant white-painted walls of the main block. The Hemis Festival (see p. 145) is held every year either in the second half of June or early in July.

Thiksey Gompa
En route to Hemis, this monastery provides a panoramic view of the Indus Valley from the top of its hill. There are 100 resident lamas and, some say, there is a nunnery too!

Shey Palace and Gompa
Also on the way to Hemis, and 15 km (9 miles) from Leh, is this summer palace of the erstwhile Raja of Leh. It is set atop a hill and houses the largest golden stupa (a memorial shrine). There is an enormous two-storied statue of Buddha in copper and gold which is well worth seeing and is quite unique. This monastery prefers visitors to make arrangements with the head lama before going out there, so, check at the Tourist Office in Leh beforehand.

Sankar Gompa
This is only 3 km (2 miles) from Leh and a nice excuse for a morning walk. One can go in the evening, too, as this monastery has electricity. There is a large collection of statues of pure gold and many interesting paintings.

Spituk Gompa
On the road just before Leh this monastery is situated on a hilltop overlooking the Indus. There is a special chamber here in which are kept enormous statues of Kali Mata, whose faces are covered and only unveiled once a year during the Spituk festival held, alas, in wintertime.

Phyang Gompa
The monastery of the red sect of Buddhists is 20 km (12 miles) on the Srinagar–Leh road. A summer festival is held here.

Alchi and Likir Gompas
In these two monasteries on the Srinagar–Leh road near Saspol are housed a number of gigantic clay statues of Buddha in various forms. The primary attraction of these monasteries is their 1000 year-old wall paintings.

Lamayuru Gompa (see section on Trekking)
Lamayuru is at the highest point on the Srinagar–Leh road. Here are mysterious caves carved out of the mountainside. It is a lonely spot, especially under the scorching summer sun.

Mulbekh Gompa

A huge image of Buddha is carved out of rock right on the roadside. The monastery is perched high on a rock above the village of Mulbekh, which is on the way to Namika-La from Leh.

Festivals

The monasteries of Ladakh are the centres for the continuance of their cultural traditions. The festivals generally follow the lunar calendar and therefore their dates vary from year to year. The most famous festival is called Hemis, after the biggest monastery of Ladakh. People from all over the area gather at Hemis to attend the festivities. The actual festival is preceded by seven days' prayers by the monks in the monastery. The most impressive and colourful part of this festival is the famous mask dance which lamas perform continuously for two days. The masks are weird, with large open mouths and have pointed teeth, bulging eyes and are surmounted by skulls. They are in red and black and yellow and they represent various gods and demons. The festival celebrates the triumph of good over evil and the actual day marks the birthday of the founder of the red sect of Buddhists, Guru Padmasambhava. This festival is held in June/July.

Other festivals are: Leh Festival – January/February; Stok Festival – February; Matho Festival – February; Lamayuru Festival – April/May; Phyang Festival – July/August; Ladakh Festival – 1st August–7th August; Thiksey Festival – September.

Kargil

Kargil stands at 2740 m (8987 ft) above sea level and 204 km (127 miles) from Srinagar, and is the second largest town in Ladakh. Once a busy meeting place of traders of all nations and religions, it is now a quiet and peaceful place where it is difficult to imagine the hundreds of caravans carrying goods like silk, ivory, jewels, carpets and spices from China, Turkey, Afghanistan and India, milling around the caravanserais and bartering their goods. These caravanserais can still be seen but are crumbling with the decay of years of neglect. There are, though, many travellers passing through Kargil during the summer season, some making a night halt *en route* to Leh, and there are facilities for their comfort.

All around are lush green fields of barley and wheat and there are

A monastery at Leh

High-altitude hillsides for grazing

vegetable beds and rows of poplars and willow trees. Kargil is famous for its mulberries and apricots, blossoming in June.

In Kargil there are some excellent examples of Turkish architecture. Day excursions can be taken to the Suru Valley nearer to the grandeur of the Himalayas where all around are lovely walks. It is so beguiling here that one is tempted to stay and not travel on to the arid regions that prevail around Leh and the upper reaches. Here live some people called the Minaros, a tribe that claims descent from the army of Alexander the Great.

There are quite a few hotels and many restaurants and there is dormitory accommodation. One can eat Chinese, Indian, Kashmiri or Western food. Buses travel here from Srinagar on the Srinagar–Leh route, and from Kashmir it is possible to have a return-the-same-day trip by jeep.

Drass

This is a small township, 60 km (37 miles) short of Kargil on the Srinagar–Leh highway, and, at 3230 m (10,594 ft) above sea level, Drass is reputed to be the coldest inhabited place in the world. Temperatures often go down to minus 40 degrees centigrade in winter.

Hill bridge, easily repaired after winter snows and flooding

Summers are just the opposite – warm and fine. The inhabitants are of the Dard stock, an Aryan race believed to have originated from Central Asia. The Dards play a sort of polo and seem to thrive, instead of just survive, in their harsh environment. Buses go from Kargil and there is a Tourist Bungalow offering accommodation.

Suru Valley

At the far end of this beautiful valley rise the Nun (7135 m [23,403 ft]) and the Kun (7035 m [23,075 ft]), twin Himalayan peaks whose glaciers slide down to the valley bed. It is a fertile valley with small farms, quite isolated yet bound by the community that lives there, the Dards, who once were Buddhist and now practice Mohammedism.

Sankoo is a small township set among forests of poplars, willows and myrtles, with verdant slopes offset by rocky mountainsides which can be dangerous to the careless foot. The mosques are a blend of Turkish and Tibetan style and seem to fuse the two religions of Buddhism and Islam.

Ladakhi novitiate

Sankoo is a good place from which to commence trekking in the region. There is a daily bus service connecting Sankoo with Kargil. Accommodation is available at modest hotels or the Government Rest House.

Zanskar

Spread over 5000 sq. km (1930 sq. miles), Zanskar is sparsely populated, the majority of people being of Indo-Tibetan origin. It is a very isolated place only recently opened up for travellers and these must be really keen. Its inaccessibility and the esoteric nature of the Buddhism practised there encourages its inhabitants to preserve their unique identity. Zanskar is one of the least-visited places in Ladakh; gradually, though, it will become a part of a regular touring of the region and one can only hope that this intrusion will be a long time away.

Once the capital of the ancient kingdom of Zanskar, Padum is now the headquarters of the region. There are several monasteries around Padum, a palace and fort and eighth-century carvings seen by the river.

For trekking and walking around this rarified region one should take a guide. It is very remote and the climate can change suddenly. Only locals

Kashmiri mother and daughter

Local shepherd gazes over hill valley above Srinagar

know how to react to these natural hazards. Warm clothing is necessary as is much planning ahead, by reading all available books on the region, so that one is quite familiar with the pitfalls as well as the pleasures of such a beautiful and intriguing region.

All information and help in planning a visit to the whole region of Ladakh can be had from the Tourist Reception Centre at Srinagar, which will advise on accommodation and suitability of weather conditions and will have accurate and detailed maps of the region.

Glossary

When compiling a glossary of words used in India and throughout the State of Jammu and Kashmir in particular, there is the multiplicity of languages to consider plus the wide use of English.

The word for sugar will be 'sugar' in one area and 'chinny' in another and 'sacar' in yet another. In Kashmir the English form will be most used for visitors, the English language tradition being a part of the culture of Kashmir for decades; in fact educated Kashmiri's speak extremely good English.

Religion

Acharaya	Teacher or spiritual guide
Ahisma	Non-violence
Ashram	Saintly place of learning
Avatar	Name given to various incarnations of Vishnu
Bhagavad Gita	Part of the Mahabharata (q.v.)
Bodhisatva	Follower of Buddha
Bo tree	*Ficus religosa*, type of banyan
Brahma	Hindu creator of all things
Brahmin	Priestly and first caste in Hinduism
Caste	Hindu hereditary class system
Dharamsala	Religious rest house without amenities
Dharma	The path of earthly conduct
Fakir	Muslim or Hindu religious mendicant
Gompa	Monastery
Granth Sahib	Sacred book of the Sikhs
Guru	Spiritual teacher
Haji	Muslim who has made the pilgrimage to Mecca
Harijan	Below caste, previously Untouchable
Imam	Muslim religious leader
Imambara	Tomb of a Shi'ite holy man
Juggernauts	Huge decorated temple carts

Kshastria	Warrior caste, second caste in Hinduism
Lama	Tibetan Buddhist priest
Lingam	Phallic symbol of Siva
Mahabharata	Principal Hindu holy book
Mantra	Word or sentence used as invocation
Muezzin	One who calls Muslims to prayer
Mullah	Muslim priest
Nirvanah	State of total peace
Pooja	Prayer before the Gods
Prasad	Food of the Gods
Qur'an	The Koran, Muslim holy book
Rath	Temple chariot
Rishi	Holy man
Sadhu	Celibate holy man
Shakti	Life force through spirituality
Sudra	Fourth and lowest Hindu caste
Sufi	Muslim mystic
Swami	Teacher within Hinduism
Tantric Buddhism	Buddhism with sexual and occult overtones
Thanka	Tibetan painting on cloth
Upanishads	Ancient Vedic scriptures
Vedas	Four most ancient Hindu writings
Yatra	Pilgrimage
Yoga	Discipline of exercise and meditation
Yoni	Female fertility symbol.

Architecture

Bagh	A garden
Bund	Embankment of a river
Chaitya	Buddhist temple or prayer hall
Chatri	Tomb or mausoleum
Darwaza	Gateway to a city, or simply a door
Diwan-i-Am	Hall of public audience
Diwan-i-Khas	Hall of private audience
Ghat	Steps leading down to water; hill sides
Gopuram	Pyramidical gateway to a temple
Mahal	Palace
Maidan	Open space, generally grassed
Mandir	Hindu temple
Masjid	Muslim mosque
Math	Monastery
Ojila	Muslim fort

Pagoda	Buddhist monument, known as stupa, dagoba or chedi
Punkah	Ceiling fan pulled by rope; used to describe electric fan
Serai	Cheap accommodation for travellers
Stupa	Buddhist sacred mound
Tank	Water storage lake
Zenana	Secluded place for women in Muslim house

Food and drink

Alu	Potato
Anda	Egg
Atta	Wholemeal flour
Biryani	Layers of partly boiled rice between which are put meat or vegetables
Chai	Tea
Chapati	Bread made of unfermented wheat dough
Chat	Name for snacks
Chini	Sugar
Dansak	Parsee preparation of rice and curried meats
Dhal	Lentils cooked in a variety of ways
Dood	Milk
Dopiaza	Meat in a thick sauce twice-boiled with lots of onions
Firnee	Creamy pudding of rice flour, milk and various nuts
Ghee	Clarified butter
Gulab jamun	Sweet balls of curd in rose syrup
Halwa	Sweetmeat made from pumpkins or carrots with sugar and milk
Jalebi	Convoluted deep-fried pancake mixture steeped in boiling flavoured sugar
Keema	Minced meat
Kheer	Sweet milk pudding
Kofta	Minced meat or vegetable balls in sauce
Korma	Thick curry enriched with ground poppy seeds and coconut
Lassi	Drink made from yoghurt and water plus flavouring
Machli	Fish
Makkhan	Butter
Masala	Condiments and spices
Murghi	Chicken
Muttar	Peas
Nan	Bread baked in tandoor oven

Pani	Water
Paneer	Cheese
Parotha	Fried bread made from wheat flour
Pulao	Rice fried in ghee and then cooked in stock
Raita	Raw vegetables chopped and mixed with yoghurt
Ras gulla	Sweet milky balls in cardamon sauce
Rogan Josh	Curried mutton or lamb
Shah Jahani	Dish garnished with silver leaf
Tandoor	Deep clay oven stoked with charcoal

Words used around Kashmir

Begum	Muslim lady of high rank
Bund	Walk by the river
Burquah	Overall covering for Muslim woman
Chappals	Sandals
Charpoi	Indian rope bed
Chenar	Type of tree seen all around the lakes
Choli	Blouse worn as undergarment by women
Chowk	Market place
Dawa	Medicine
Doonga	Domestic houseboat
Durbar	Royal court
Gaddi	Throne of royalty
Ghari	Carriage or motor vehicle
Ghazal	Urdu love song
Hanji	Shikara paddler
Hookah	Hubble-bubble water pipe for smoking tobacco
Kangra	Basket, round, lined with clay and heated with charcoal and used for personal heating. Men and women sit with this beneath their voluminous clothes. Too much of this heat can induce stomach cancer and does produce heat-weals on the flesh
Kameeze	Trouser-like garment worn by Muslim men and women
Lakh	Of rupees, equals 100,000
Lathi	Indian policeman's control stick
Mali	Gardener
Mantra	Prayer
Mela	Fair or festival
Nawab	Governor
Numda	Wool rug on which there is embroidery work
Peon	Lower grade clerical worker

Pashmina	Type of shawl woven from the fleece of the under-belly of the Pashmina goat
Phul	Flower
Raga	Theme for musical variations
Rajput	Hindu warrior of Rajasthan
Salwar	Blouse worn by Muslim and Hindu women according to fashion
Shikara	Small punt paddled over the waters of the Kashmiri lakes
Zamindar	Rich landowner

Further reading

ARCHER, M.   *Indian Architecture and the British*   Thames & Hudson   1976

COLLINS, J. & LAPIERE, D.   *Freedom at Midnight*   Collins   1975

CRAVEN, R.C.   *Concise History of Indian Art*   Thames & Hudson   1976

DROUBIE, R. EL   *Islam*   Ward Lock Educational   1970

EDWARDS, M.   *Indian Temples and Palaces*   Hamlyn   1969

FISHLOCK, T.   *India File*   Murray   1983

GASCOIGNE, B.   *The Great Moghuls*   Cape   1971

GRANT, W.J.   *Spirit of India*   Batsford   1938

HAMBLEY, G.   *Cities of Mughal India*   Elek   1968

HUTTON, J.H.   *Caste in India*   CUP   1946

IONS, V.   *Myths and Legends of India*   Hamlyn   1970

MEHTA, V.   *Portrait of India*   Penguin   1950

MOORHOUSE, G.   *India Britannica*   Harvil Press   1982

NAIPAUL, V.S.   *An Area of Darkness*   Deutsche   1964

PANDEY, B.N.   *A Book of India*   Collins   1981

RAWSON, P.   *Indian Asia*   Elsevier–Phaidon   1977

RUSHBROOK WILLIAMS, L.F.   *A Handbook for Travellers in India* (etc)   Murray   1958

SEN, K.M.   *Hinduism*   Pelican   1961

SINGH, R.   *Kashmir, Garden of the Himalayas*   Perennial Press   1983

SMITH, V.A.   *The Oxford History of India* (3rd edition)   OUP   1958

SPEAR, SIR P.   *Twilight of the Moghuls*   CUP   1951

WOODCOCK, G.   *Faces of India*   Faber   1967

YOUNGHUSBAND, SIR FRANCIS   *Kashmir*   A & C Black   1917

Index